Tantalizing Tidbits for Middle Schoolers:

Quick Booktalks for the Busy Middle School and Jr. High Library Media Specialist

By Ruth E. Cox Clark, Ph.D.

Professional Development Resources for K-12
Library Media and Technology Specialists

Library of Congress Cataloging-in-Publication Data

Cox Clark, Ruth E.
  Tantalizing tidbits for middle schoolers : quick booktalks for the busy middle school and jr. high library media specialist / Ruth E. Cox Clark.
    p. cm.
  Includes indexes.
  ISBN 1-58683-195-X (pbk.)
 1. Book talks--United States. 2. Middle school libraries--Activity programs--United States. 3. Junior high school libraries--Activity programs--United States. 4. Preteens--Books and reading--United States. 5. Teenagers--Books and reading--United States. 6. Children's literature--Bibliography. 7. Young adult literature--Bibliography. I. Title.
Z1003.15.C69 2005
028.5'5--dc22
                                2005013159

Author: Ruth E. Cox Clark

Linworth Books:
Carol Simpson, Editorial Director
Judi Repman, Associate Editor

Published by Linworth Publishing, Inc.
480 East Wilson Bridge Road, Suite L
Worthington, Ohio 43085

Copyright © 2005 by Linworth Publishing, Inc.

All rights reserved. Purchasing this book entitles a librarian to reproduce activity sheets for use in the library within a school or entitles a teacher to reproduce activity sheets for single classroom use within a school. Other portions of the book (up to 15 pages) may be copied for staff development purposes within a single school. Standard citation information should appear on each page. The reproduction of any part of this book for an entire school or school system or for commercial use is strictly prohibited. No part of this book may be electronically reproduced, transmitted, or recorded without written permission from the publisher.

ISBN 1-58683-195-X

Table of Contents

About the Author v

Dedication v

Section 1. Introduction 1
    Audience 1
    Book Entry Format 2
        Bibliographic Information 2
        Web Site 2
        Subjects 3
        Genres 3
        Awards 3
        Lists 3
        Levels 4
        Annotation 4
        Booktalk 4
        Excerpt 5
        Curriculum Connections 5
        Similar Titles 5
    Collaboration with Classroom Teachers 6

Section 2. Annual Recommended Reading Lists 7
    The Association of Library Services to Children (ALSC) Lists ... 7
        Notable Children's Books 7
    The International Reading Association (IRA) Lists 8
        Children's Choices 8
        Teachers' Choices 8
        Young Adults' Choices 9
    The Young Adult Library Services Association (YALSA) Lists 9
        Best Books for Young Adults 9
        Quick Picks for Reluctant Young Adult Readers 9

Section 3. Awards 11
    Michael L. Printz Award 11
    John Newbery Award 11
    Coretta Scott King Award 12

Section 4. Booktalking Techniques ... 13
Booktalking Styles ... 13
Excerpt ... 13
Narrative ... 14
First Person ... 14
Before and After the Booktalk ... 15

Section 5. Booktalks ... 19

Section 6. Indices ... 113
Author ... 113
Authors, Similar Titles ... 115
Titles ... 124
Titles, Similar ... 126
Subjects ... 135
Genres ... 137
Curriculum Connections ... 138

Section 7. Appendix: Student Evaluation Form ... 139

About the Author

Ruth E. Cox Clark is a part-time online faculty member for the University of Houston-Clear Lake (UHCL), School of Education, teaching graduate and undergraduate level Young Adult Literature courses. She is also the Librarian for the Virgin Islands Montessori School on the island of St. Thomas in the U.S. Virgin Islands. While a full-time faculty member at UHCL, she taught other university level courses including Children's Literature and Administration of School Library Media Centers courses, as well as supervised the School Library Internships. Her previously held positions include an Assistant Professorship at Sam Houston State University in the Masters in Library Science Program, a School District Library Services Directorship in Wisconsin, as well as various K-12 building-level school library media specialist positions in Alaska and Texas. Literature committee appointments include the Young Adult Library Services Association's Best Books for Young Adults and the Printz Award committees as well as the Association of Library Services for Children's Newbery Award committee. She has also been the Chair of the Educators of Library Media Specialists Section within the American Association of School Librarians and the President of the Wisconsin Association of School Librarians.

Dedication

To Drs. Maureen White and Peg Hill, the two best mentors anyone could ask for. Thanks for all the professional and moral support.

Introduction

Tantalizing Tidbits for Middle Schoolers is a professional resource to assist middle and junior high school library media specialists in introducing leisure reading titles to students, as well as to provide short booktalks for curriculum-related titles.

Although the target audience for *Tantalizing Tidbits for Middle Schoolers* is library media specialists, classroom teachers will find the curriculum-related activities useful.

A. Audience

The titles included in *Tantalizing Tidbits for Middle Schoolers* are appropriate for fifth through eighth grade library media center collections, based on professional review recommendations. Books with reviews that list ninth grade as the lowest recommended interest level are not included in this collection of booktalks because many school districts consider ninth grade as a high school grade level. The intent is to provide booktalks that will appeal to middle and junior high school readers, ages 10 through 13.

As is the case for books intended for any age group of readers, some of the chosen books may be considered controversial. Please keep in mind that there is a considerable difference between what is appropriate for the mature eighth grade reader versus the younger fifth grade reader. Not all of the 75 booktalked books, or the additional 375 similar titles, are appropriate for all grade levels within the fifth through eighth grade range. The final decision is in the hands of the booktalker.

To further ensure that the included books are recommended for middle school and/or junior high library media centers, along with having appropriate suggested interest levels in professional reviews, many are on the American Library Association and/or the International Reading Association recommended reading lists that target younger teens. For example, the American Association of Library Services to Children (ALSC) Notable Children's Books list includes a section for "Older Readers" in which a number of the booktalked titles are included.

B. Book Entry Format

The 75 entries in *Tantalizing Tidbits for Middle Schoolers* are similarly formatted, but may vary in the number of elements included. For example, if a book has not received the Printz, Newbery, or Coretta Scott King award, or has not been selected for inclusion on one of six recommended book lists examined, these elements will not be included in the entry. Please be aware that the entry information is based on when *Tantalizing Tidbits for Middle Schoolers* is published. Editions of books included may have gone out of print, new editions may have become available, and/or the title may appear on recommended reading lists or have journal reviews that are not listed. The title entry elements are described below.

1. Bibliographic Information

Each entry begins with the basic bibliographic information for readily available editions that are currently in print. It is not unusual for a popular children's or young adult title to be out of print in hardback, but to stay in paperback print for many years, with numerous reprints and new cover art appearing. Whenever possible the most current hardback and paperback editions are listed, in that order, followed by the audio books, tapes first, then CDs. ISBNs and prices are included to assist in the purchasing process. In print status has been checked against the online version of *Books in Print* at <www.BooksInPrint.com>.

2. Web Site

Author Web sites are listed when available. There are many online resources that include author information, such as publishers' Web sites, but only those specific to the author, or the title/series such as Angie Sage's *Magyk,* are listed. These sites can be shared with teachers and students by bookmarking them on the library media center computers. Ready access to current author information will increase students' awareness of other titles by an author. Many of the author sites also have a link for students to email the author. Be aware that URLs change frequently as does the content; therefore, any bookmarked sites should be checked on a regular basis.

3. Subjects

A minimum of one subject area is listed for each entry. These are not Library of Congress subject headings, but are subject-related terms frequently used by teachers or students when they visit the library media center requesting books to support the curriculum or for their leisure reading needs. For example, a history teacher will most likely ask for books on World War II rather than using the proper Library of Congress subject heading of "World War, 1939-1945."

4. Genres

Along with subject and curriculum requests, library media specialists often receive requests for books in a specific genre. For example, a Social Studies teacher may request a booktalk on historical fiction titles specific to the time period being studied. Please be aware that no attempt has been made to balance the number of books by genre in *Tantalizing Tidbits for Middle Schoolers*. The titles were chosen for middle and junior high library media center collection suitability and ease of booktalking.

5. Awards

Books that have received the Michael L. Printz, John Newbery, and/or Coretta Scott King awards are noted as such in the entry. These awards honor both children's and young adult books. Please see Section 3 for a description of each of the awards.

6. Lists

A number of the titles included in *Tantalizing Tidbits for Middle Schoolers* have been chosen by children's and/or young adult literature professionals for association sponsored book lists. Many of the non-list titles were nominated but did not make the final vote or are titles that are too new to be on recommended book lists.

The ALA and/or IRA book list and year of inclusion are listed. Some books will appear on more than one list. For example, a title may appear on the YALSA Best Books for Young Adults list as well as the ALSC Notable Children's Books list because of the two-year overlap in the associations' definitions of children (ages birth to 14) and young adults (ages 12 through 18). Titles were checked against the ALA lists up through 2005, which includes books published in 2004.

The IRA Young Adults' Choices, Children's Choices, and Teacher's Choices lists were also checked for title inclusion, through the 2004 lists. For these lists teens, children, and teachers in selected U.S. schools vote for their favorite books, rather than professionals choosing titles for recommended reading lists, as is the case for the ALA lists. Section 2 includes a description of the book lists.

7. Levels

The interest levels listed are grade levels. For some of the review journals ages have been converted to grade levels. For example, age 10 has been converted to fifth grade and age 13 to eighth grade. The recommended interest levels do not all include a range of middle school grades only. They may state 7 up, meaning the suggested interest level is seventh grade and higher. The selection criteria for the books in *Tantalizing Tidbits for Middle Schoolers* does not preclude including those titles suggested for grade levels above or below grades five through eight, but the suggested interest range must include at least two of these grade levels. Please note that reviewer suggested interest levels are just that, suggestions. The suggested grade level ranges among the review journals may, and often do, vary considerably. The school library media specialist makes the final decision for inclusion in a collection or determines the appropriateness of the title for a booktalk.

The grade level interest information has been confirmed in *Booklist, Kirkus Review, Library Journal, Library Media Connection, Publishers' Weekly, School Library Journal,* and/or *Voice of Youth Advocates (VOYA)*. Whenever possible, more than one review source is listed. The following online sources were used to locate the review interest level information: <www.amazon.com>, <www.barnesandnoble.com>, <www.booksinprint.com>, and <www.titlewave.com>.

8. Annotation

An annotation is included for each entry because booktalks are meant to entice, not to tell the whole story. Unlike the potential middle or junior high school reader, the library media specialist selecting titles to booktalk and/or add to the collection needs more information about the book's content than a booktalk can, or should, give. The annotation includes, along with a basic plot summary, the age of the protagonist and the setting whenever possible. Please keep in mind that the age of a protagonist does not always relate to the reader interest level of a book. For example, Christopher Paul Curtis' Newbery and Coretta Scott King award-winning title, *Bud, Not Buddy*, has a 10-year-old protagonist. Although Bud is quite young, his experiences are ones that readers of many ages can relate to, certainly those of middle and junior high school age.

9. Booktalk

A short attention getting booktalk in first person or narrative style is included. Please see Section 4: Booktalking Techniques for further information on the different styles of booktalks, as well as other hints for preparing and presenting booktalks.

10. Excerpt

A page range of text that may be used in an excerpt style booktalk is included. The pages listed are from the hardback edition of the book unless otherwise noted. The suggested excerpts are included as an additional quick way for library media specialists to highlight the book.

11. Curriculum Connections

Middle/junior high school curriculum areas are listed for each entry, with a suggested extension activity for students. The curriculum-related extension activities include a research element to ensure library media center involvement. The school library media specialist should be an integral part of the school faculty and these curriculum-related extension activities will encourage collaboration between the classroom teacher and the library media specialist.

12. Similar Titles

A list of five author, genre, or subject area similar titles concludes each entry. The suggested titles may include both nonfiction and fiction titles. General bibliographic information is included for each of the 375 similar titles, but library media specialists will need to check for suitability for their particular library media center and booktalking audience. These similar titles range in suggested interest level, from lower level informational books to supplement knowledge about the subject, to novels intended for the older middle school student.

    The similar titles do not include any books with entries in *Tantalizing Tidbits for Middle Schoolers*. Nor do any of the similar titles appear in more than one entry. The intent of including a list of similar titles is to assist the school library media specialist in quickly pulling together a group of books to supplement titles being booktalked to ensure there will be an adequate number of book choices for the students. For example, booktalking five titles from *Tantalizing Tidbits for Teens* will result in an additional 25 books similar in nature (author, genre, or subject) that can be offered to the students. These titles can also be used to assist in reader's advisory services, even when booktalking has not taken place.

    Some of the similar titles are newly published, but many of them are well-known and/or older titles. For example, *Friction* by E.R. Frank is a 2003 title, but the similar titles list ranges in publication date from 1975 to 2002. The familiar older titles have been included because many of these titles may already be in middle and/or junior high school library media centers. Even if a paperback edition is listed as the only edition currently available, the original hardback edition of an older title may be in the collection.

C. Collaboration with Classroom Teachers

The curriculum connection and subject information is included for each book to assist the library media specialist in putting together booktalking sessions of various types. The library media specialist may browse through *Tantalizing Tidbits for Middle Schoolers* to find booktalks to introduce students to a wide variety of books. The specific entry information and the indices may be used to select titles for curriculum-related booktalking sessions. Browsing through and reading booktalks that look interesting is an excellent way to become familiar with this booktalking resource, but the author, title, subject, genre, and curriculum connection indices greatly enhance its usability.

Tantalizing Tidbits for Middle Schoolers should be shared with teachers. The entries include curriculum-related extension activities for students. Integrating literature into the curriculum and helping create lifelong readers are part of what teachers and library media specialists do on a daily basis. The curriculum connection activities for these novels suggest ways for library media specialists and teachers to help students make the connection between an enjoyable reading experience and possible research activities that relate to the character, setting, or plot of the story, extending the reading experience into other areas of the curriculum.

Annual Recommended Reading Lists

Thousands of books are published each year in the United States. A much smaller number of these titles appear on association-created recommended book lists. A number of the titles selected for inclusion in *Tantalizing Tidbits for Middle Schoolers* are titles chosen by professionals for YALSA's Best Books for Young Adults and Quick Picks for Reluctant Young Adult Readers lists, ALSC's Notable Children's, and/or by the student and teacher self-selected IRA Young Adults' Choices, Children's Choices, and Teacher's Choices lists.

A. The Association of Library Services to Children (ALSC) Lists

Although the Association of Library Services to Children produces a number of annual book lists, Notable Children's Books is the ALSC-sponsored list relevant to the titles included in *Tantalizing Tidbits for Middle Schoolers*.

1. Notable Children's Books

The titles on the Notable Children's Books list are chosen by a committee of professionals in the area of children's literature who are members of the Association of Library Services to Children (ALSC), a division of the American Library Association (ALA). The committee selects an annual list of notable children's books chosen from the thousands of titles published in the United States during the previous year. The list is divided up into three levels: younger readers, middle readers, and older readers. The titles for middle and older readers include books appropriate for middle and junior high school readers and were checked for booktalked titles included in *Tantalizing Tidbits for Middle Schoolers*. The recent Notable Children's Books annual lists are available at <http://www.ala.org/Content/NavigationMenu/ALSC/Awards_and_Scholarships1/Childrens_Notable_Lists/Default1888.htm>.

B. The International Reading Association (IRA) Lists

The International Reading Association works with reading and library professionals and students in both elementary and secondary schools throughout the United States to create the annual Children's Choices, Young Adults' Choices, and Teachers' Choices lists. The participants in the chosen schools vote for their favorite books and the votes are tallied. The books receiving the most votes make the annual lists.

1. Children's Choices

Children from around the United States choose approximately 100 books, fiction and nonfiction, for the annual Children's Choices list. This is a joint project between the International Reading Association and the Children's Book Council. Team leaders from five different regions of the United States choose schools within their areas to receive books marketed for children. Throughout the school year the books are shared with students both in the classroom and in the library media center. The titles on the list are divided into those for beginning readers (ages 5-6), young readers (ages 6-8), intermediate readers (ages 8-10), and advanced readers (ages 10-13). Titles listed for the oldest group of readers, the advanced readers, target the middle school and junior high school age readers. The Children's Choices list is available at <http://www.reading.org/choices>.

2. Teachers' Choices

Teachers and librarians from around the United States choose the approximately 30 books on the annual Teachers' Choices list. Seven regional coordinators circulate copies of the books to teachers and librarians who then share them with students. Each book is read by a minimum of six teachers and/or library media specialists within each of the seven regional areas. The titles on the list are divided up into primary (K-2, ages 5-8), intermediate (grades 3-5, ages 8-11), and advanced (grades 6-8, ages 11-14). Titles intended for the oldest group of readers, the advanced readers, targets the middle school and junior high school age readers. The Teachers' Choices list is available at <http://www.reading.org/choices>.

3. Young Adults' Choices

Teen readers from around the United States choose 30 books for the annual Young Adults' Choices list. Each year the International Reading Association selects team leaders from five different regions of the United States. The team leaders then choose several secondary schools within their areas to receive books marketed for young adults, ages 12 through 18. Publishers send books, which have received two positive reviews in recognized review journals, to the team leaders who then coordinate the placement of the books in the participating schools. The teens self-select what they want to read, voting on their favorites. The 30 books, fiction or nonfiction, with the most votes become the list, which is then annotated by the members of the Literature for Young Adults Committee. The results are announced at the International Reading Association National Conference in May. Recent years' Young Adults' Choices lists are available at <http://www.reading.org/choices/choices_download.html>.

C. The Young Adult Library Services Association (YALSA) Lists

The titles on the Best Books for Young Adults and the Quick Picks for Reluctant Young Adult Readers lists are chosen by committees of professionals in the area of young adult literature who are members of the Young Adult Library Services Association (YALSA), a division of the American Library Association (ALA). The publishers' intended audience for all of the books on these lists may not be teens, but the committee considers the listed titles appropriate and recommended for teens ages 12 through 18. Although these lists are intended for a broader range of teen readers than is addressed in *Tantalizing Tidbits for Middle Schoolers*, the interest level recommendations from the reviews journals eliminated from inclusion those titles intended for the older teen audience. Information about the Young Adult Library Services Association is available at <http://www.ala.org/Content/NavigationMenu/YALSA/YALSA.htm>.

1. The Best Books for Young Adults

The Best Books for Young Adults annual list includes fiction and nonfiction books published within the previous 16 months and recommended for teens within the age range of 12 through 18. The lists are available at <http://www.ala.org/Content/NavigationMenu/YALSA/Booklists_and_Book_Awards/Best_Books_for_Young_Adults/Best_Books_for_Young_Adults.htm>.

2. Quick Picks for Reluctant Young Adult Readers

The Quick Picks for Reluctant Young Adult Readers committee prepares an annual annotated list of books published in the last 18 months that are recommended reading for reluctant teen readers. These titles are intended for recreational reading, not for remedial or curricular use. The titles should have self-selection appeal to teens, ages 12 through

18. The subject matter, cover art, readability, format, and style are considered when nominating and voting on titles. The lists are available at <http://www.ala.org/Content/ NavigationMenu/YALSA/Booklists_and_ Book_Awards/Quick_Picks_for_Reluctant_Young_Adult_Readers/Quick_ Picks_for_Reluctant_Young_Adult_Readers.htm>.

Awards

The awards discussed in this section are sponsored by divisions and a round table within the American Library Association. The intended audience of the books that have won these awards is broader than grades five through eight. The award-created categories, as well as the recommended interest levels in the review journals, have been used to help choose titles appropriate for *Tantalizing Tidbits for Middle Schoolers*.

A. Michael L. Printz Award

The Michael L. Printz Award recognizes literary excellence in young adult literature. A nine-member selection committee names one award book and as many as four honor books on an annual basis. The books must have been published between January 1 and December 31 of the prior year and be designated as a young adult book by the publisher or published for the age range of 12 through 18. The books may be fiction, nonfiction, poetry, or an anthology and may have been previously published in another country. More information about this award can be found at <http://www.ala.org/Template.cfm? Section=Book_Media_Awards&template=/ContentManagement/ContentDisplay.cfm&ContentID=26634>.

B. John Newbery Award

The Association of Library Services to Children annually presents the John Newbery Award, which recognizes literary excellence. A 15-member committee chooses the most distinguished book for children (ages birth through 14) published in English in the United States during the preceding year. Honor books are also chosen, typically between one and four titles.

Although the award is sponsored by the Association of Library Services to Children, rather than the Young Adult Library Services Association, quite frequently the titles chosen for this award are at the upper end of the age range, 12 to 14. Due to the two-year overlap, 12 through 14, in the definition of children (ages birth through 14) and young adults (ages 12 through 18), the Newbery award and honor books are frequently of interest to middle and junior high school students. A list of the award and honor books is available at <http://www.ala.org/ala/alsc/ awardsscholarships/literaryawds/ newberymedal/newberymedal.htm>.

C. Coretta Scott King Award

The Coretta Scott King Task Force of the American Library Association's Social Responsibilities Round Table presents the Coretta Scott King Award annually. The purpose of this award is to encourage the expression of the African-American experience through literature and the graphic arts. The author or illustrator must be African American and the book must portray an aspect of the black experience.

A seven-member award committee chooses annual author and illustrator awards. The award-winning titles must be written for children and/or young adults within the three following categories: preschool-grade 4, grades 6-8, and grades 9-12. The middle category, grades 6-8, targets the middle and junior high school audience and was examined for booktalked titles included in *Tantalizing Tidbits for Middle Schoolers*. More information about this award can be found at <http://www.ala.org/ala/emiert/corettascottkingbookawards/corettascott.htm>.

Booktalking Techniques

Booktalking is much like acting, but in this case the booktalker is also the writer, the producer, and the director. There is no off scene director shouting, "Cut!" if the booktalker deviates from the "script." Some booktalkers work from outlines or notes and others have actual "scripts" that they memorize. There is no right or wrong way to prepare for a booktalk, but preparation is a must. It is not wise to booktalk a book that hasn't been read, or one that cannot be recommended. A student who enjoyed reading a booktalked book may want to discuss it with the library media specialist. Reading the book, and similar titles to recommend, ensures that the follow-up discussion is satisfying for both the reader and the library media specialist.

A. Booktalking Styles

Booktalks are as unique as the person presenting them, but basically there are three styles of booktalks most often used – the excerpt, the narrative, and the first person.

1. Excerpt

The excerpt is the easiest – find an intriguing tidbit of text and read it aloud to the students, leaving them with a cliffhanger. The excerpt should have the audience wanting more – wondering what happens next. When reading a book, keep page flags available to mark passages for future booktalks. Remember to also write the page number(s) down elsewhere, since the book being shared will more than likely be checked out at the conclusion of the booktalk. The excerpt style of booktalk is not included in *Tantalizing Tidbits for Middle Schoolers*, but each entry lists a suggested section of text that may be used in an excerpt style booktalk.

Excerpts should not be long because while reading the booktalker's head is down and eye contact with the students is lost. Eye contact is an essential part of booktalking as it helps the booktalker "read" students' responses to the booktalk to help in determining whether to cut this one short, to expand upon it, or to elicit student input to increase their involvement.

2. Narrative

The narrative booktalk takes a bit more work on the booktalker's part. The booktalker shares tidbits about the plot, setting, character, or an intriguing incident from the book to get the potential readers' attention. Asking a question also helps pull students into this style of booktalk.

For example, while booktalking Jerry Spinelli's *Loser*, a booktalker may begin with: "Do any of you have a nickname that you don't like? I see some of you nodding your heads and grimacing. The guy in this book has a nickname his classmates gave him and it isn't one any of you would want to have. It is a very mean nickname. The problem is – Zinkoff is the kind of kid who just brings it on himself, without even realizing it. He has no clue how irritating he can be. Sadly, sometimes he really *is* a Loser."

The booktalker then holds up the book horizontally so that the title, *Loser,* boldly written on the spine, is clearly observable to the audience. The booktalker then shows the front cover and back cover, saying "Loser" with each movement of the book so the students can clearly see the title written on both the front and back covers of the book. The short booktalk is finished up with, "But don't feel too sorry for Zinkoff, he will prove his classmates wrong. His nickname Loser is about to be replaced by one we would all love to have."

3. First Person

The first person booktalk takes a bit of acting skill on the booktalker's part. While presenting this style of booktalk, the booktalker becomes one of the characters in the book and talks about what happened to him or her.

First person novels, such as *Friction* by E.R. Frank, allow the booktalker to readily move into a first person booktalk because of the strong narrator's voice.

"Hi. I'm Alex. Have you ever felt like your life was out of control and there was nothing you could do to stop it? That what you were doing was hurting other people and no matter what you did to try and make it better, it just got worse? The school year started out great. We have this really neat teacher, Simon, who does all kinds of science experiments with us and even takes us on camping trips. By the way, I don't go to a regular school, I go to an alternative school and I am in the 8th grade. We really do get to call our teachers by their first names. Anyway, everything was going just fine and then this new kid, Stacy, joined our class. At first I liked hanging around with her. She did and said things no one else would even think about, let alone dare say out loud. But then she started saying things about Simon and me. She said that Simon was in love with me. That's stupid. I'm just a kid and he's a man and besides, he's got a girlfriend. But Stacy wouldn't give up on it – she kept putting these doubts in my head, and then she started telling the other kids too. It's not true, but I think I let it go too far and now Simon might be in trouble. And, I'm partially to blame because I listened to Stacy's stupid lies."

Alex's strong voice makes *Friction* a perfect first person booktalking title. Working with Alex's uncertainty and guilt over what happened to Simon helps create an attention getting first person booktalk. This booktalk is relatively easy to create and present because Frank does a marvelous job of creating a realistic female character who is entering puberty with all the yearnings and uncertainties that go along with this stage of development.

Can a booktalker present first person booktalks for books in which the character is of the opposite sex? Yes, it is quite acceptable, and downright fun, to do first person booktalks for both male and female main characters. Granted, it may be somewhat of a stretch at first to do an opposite sex first person booktalk, but it can be done, and done so effectively that the students forgets the booktalker isn't the character being portrayed. In most cases the first person booktalk causes the students to sit up and pay attention as they try to figure out what the booktalker is doing. Starting a booktalking session with a first person booktalk is an effective way to engage the students immediately.

Each booktalker finds his or her unique style with practice, but it is wise to vary the types of booktalks given during a booktalking session.

B. Before and After the Booktalk

Most booktalkers write up their booktalks and the transitional statements between books before a session, but a "seasoned" booktalker rarely uses these notes while booktalking. But, if notes are necessary, the booktalker should put them where they can be easily seen without having to pick them up. Printing them in a large size font will make notes readable at a glance.

Library media specialists preparing to booktalk for the first time may want to videotape themselves so they can critique their style before they get up in front of a group of middle schoolers. Viewing themselves engaged in booktalking will help the novice booktalkers eliminate mannerisms and gestures that may distract the audience, such as the repeated use of "um," "like," and other filler words. It is also a way to practice smooth transitions between books so a booktalker is not repeating "And this book is..." before moving on to the next book.

Middle schoolers will ask questions about what happens next in the book. The idea is to get them to read the book, but ending each booktalk with, "You'll have to read the book to find out" is not a good idea. Vary the booktalk endings by making a smooth transition to the next book by relating the characters or setting of the books, tying them together as you move from book to book. Students may attempt to get the booktalker to "tell the rest of the story" but that should be avoided. If potential readers are told what happens why would they bother reading the book?

To ensure that the students remember the book being booktalked, clearly state the author and title. It is also a good idea to hand out a list of the books, with catchy attention getting one-liners for each title, before beginning the booktalking session so the students can mark the titles they are most interested in reading.

Consider putting the title of the book first, in boldface print, rather than the author's name. Doing so allows students to quickly find the book on the list. Listeners are more likely to remember the title of a book than the author. Include similar titles on the list since, in most cases, there won't be adequate copies of the booktalked titles to meet reader demand. If only one copy of a booktalked book is available, make sure to bring numerous similar titles. Each entry in *Tantalizing Tidbits for Middle Schoolers* includes a list of five similar books.

A book cart or a display of the booktalked books and similar titles alleviates the frustration that may occur when students get excited about a book but cannot check it out because of a waiting list. Also consider sharing the list of titles booktalked with the public library and the local bookstore so they will be prepared for those readers with public library cards and/or cash to buy the books.

The specific group of students and the booktalking environment will determine the length of the session. A short informal booktalk for a single book with a student may take place in the library media center, or even in the school hallway. On the other hand, booktalking may involve a lengthy prearranged booktalking session for a particular group of students. Thirty minutes is a suitable length of time to booktalk with students. Approximately 15 titles can be shared in a 30-minute session, but more books than can be booktalked should be available. A booktalker may talk faster than planned, or "reading" students' response may indicate that some of the planned booktalks are not relevant to this particular group. Also, a booktalker should allow time for the students to ask questions and to browse through the books.

Booktalks are logistically easier for the library media specialist to do in the library media center, but many teachers do not have the time to take their students there. In a large school it may take a good portion of the class period to walk to the library media center and get the students settled down for the booktalks. On the other hand, the library media specialist can be waiting in the classroom, prepared to start booktalking as soon as the students are seated. This is the library media specialist's chance to "advertise" as many books as possible. Also, visiting the classrooms gives the library media specialist additional visibility in the school.

At the conclusion of a booktalking session, the booktalker should ask the teacher and students for input. If a particular booktalk did not go over well with the audience, it may not have been the book, but rather the style of the booktalk. There is often little time for oral evaluative input when booktalking during a class period. It is a good idea to hand out an evaluation form so the students can offer specific input. See the Student Evaluation Form in the Appendix.

As soon as possible after the booktalking session a booktalker should make notes on the students' responses. The date and the group of students should be noted on the book list and/or the booktalk notes to keep from repeating a booktalk with the same students. Most booktalkers keep print or electronic copies of their booktalks. Some booktalkers use three-ring binders with a booktalk per page. Others use index cards. Many booktalkers create a Word or Excel file that can be added to as new booktalks are created and old ones are adapted.

Booktalking should be an integral part of the school library media program. Along with group booktalks, offer to do one or two during the morning announcements and design a special display for the booktalked books. If there is a TV studio in the school, offer to do booktalks on the air, as well as assist students in writing and presenting their own. Get teachers involved in doing booktalks with their students and suggest they allow time for students to booktalk in class.

Presenting booktalks is often overlooked because of the extensive use of the school library media center for curriculum-related assignments, but helping students become lifelong readers goes hand in hand with teaching information literacy skills.

Booktalks

Abbreviations used in this section:

BBYA	Best Books for Young Adults.
BL	*Booklist.*
CC	Children's Choices.
CN	Notable Children's.
K	*Kirkus Review.*
LJ	*Library Journal.*
LMC	*Library Media Connection.*
PW	*Publishers' Weekly.*
QP	Quick Picks for Reluctant Young Adult Readers.
SLJ	*School Library Journal.*
TC	Teachers' Choices.
YAC	Young Adults' Choices.

Allende, Isabel, *Kingdom of the Golden Dragon.*

HarperCollins, 2004, 437pp. $20.89. ISBN: 0060589434. HarperCollins, 2005, 464pp. $7.99. ISBN: 0060589442. HarperCollinsAudio, 2004. $29.95. ISBN: 0060597593.

Web Site: <www.isabelallende.com>
Subjects: Crime, Friendship, Grandmothers, Kidnapping, Magic, Religion
Genre: Adventure, Fantasy, International, Multicultural, Mystery
Levels: BL 7-12, K 8-10, PW 5 up, SLJ 5-8

Annotation: Alex Cold's and Nadia Santos' second adventure with Alex's grandmother, a reporter for International Geographic, is in an isolated Himalayan kingdom, where Nadia and Alex use their animal totemic powers to help a Prince and a Buddhist monk save the sacred Golden Dragon.

Booktalk: I should have known when grandmother offered to take Nadia and me with her on this trip to the Kingdom of the Golden Dragon that it wasn't going to be an ordinary trip. Nothing is ordinary with my grandmother! Last time I went on a trip with her I ended up in the Amazon where I fought off more than mosquitoes. But I also met Nadia on that trip. She still lives in South America, but Grandmother invited her along – I think to keep me out of trouble. Yeah right – Nadia is the one who gets us into trouble! Now the three of us, Grandmother, Nadia, and me, are off to a forbidden kingdom in the Himalayas. Not many people are allowed in, but my grandmother can be pretty persuasive when she wants something, and she wants a picture of the sacred Golden Dragon. Like the king is going to have it out on display! I wonder what Kate (she doesn't like to be called grandmother) has up her sleeve this time.

Excerpt: Fifth paragraph on page 6 to break on page 9.

Curriculum Connections: Health, Science
The Buddhist monks who Alex and Nadia meet are able to slow down their heart rate to the point that they are at the edge of death. Have students use library media center resources to research the relaxation methods the monks use to slow down their respiration and heart rate and discuss how these types of relaxation techniques could be useful in their own lives.

Similar Titles:
Allende, Isabel, *City of the Beasts.* HarperCollins, 2002, 416pp. $21.89. ISBN: 0060509171. HarperCollins, 2005, 464pp. $7.99. ISBN 0060776455. HarperChildrens Audio, 2002. $29.95. ISBN: 0060510765.
Bell, William, *Forbidden City: A Novel of Modern Day China.* Random House, 1996, 199pp. $5.99. ISBN: 0440226791.
Neale, Jonathan, *Himalaya.* Houghton Mifflin, 2004, 160pp. $16.00. ISBN: 061841200X.

Sis, Peter, ***Tibet Through the Red Book.*** Farrar, Straus & Giroux, 1998, 64pp. $25.00. ISBN: 0374375526.

Whitesel, Cheryl Alyward, ***Rebel: A Tibetan Odyssey.*** HarperCollins, 2000, 208pp. $16.99. ISBN: 0688167357.

Almond, David, *Skellig.*

Bantam Doubleday Dell, 1999, 182pp. $16.95. ISBN: 038532653X. Random House, 2001, 208pp. $5.99. ISBN: 0440229081. Books on Tape, 2000. $18.00. ISBN: 0736690255.

Web Site: <www.davidalmond.com>
Subjects: Family Problems, Friendship, Infants, Moving, Religion
Genre: Fantasy, International, Supernatural
Awards: 2000 Printz Honor
Lists: 2000 CN
Levels: BL 5-8, K 6-8, LJ 5-9, PW 3-7, SLJ 5-9

Annotation: Ten-year-old Michael explores the old garage next to their house while his parents spend time at the hospital with his ill infant sister. Michael and his new neighborhood friend, Mina, discover Skellig, a mysterious winged creature who they nurse back to health.

Booktalk: Michael had been excited about moving into their new home. It might be an old house much in need of repair, but it was a new home for his family. But then his baby sister became very ill and his mother was spending all her time in the hospital and his father was keeping himself so busy with working on the house that he didn't have time for Michael. So Michael began to wander. He wandered right into the dilapidated old garage his father had told him to stay out of. That is where he found … it? Him? Michael wasn't quite sure what to make of the dried up old thing covered with spider webs. There were even dead flies caught in his hair! Michael could make out what he thought were wings on the creature's back and since he was sure the creature was dead, Michael shined his flashlight into the dried up old face. That's when he heard a voice, raspy from disuse, ask, "What do you want?" Before Michael could even think to answer he heard his father calling for him and ran out of the garage worried his father would figure out what he had been up to. Remembering what he had seen and heard in the garage, Michael could not fall asleep that night. What if that thing came and found him in his bedroom when he was asleep? Michael had no way of knowing that the mysterious creature in the garage would play a major part in his life and that of his baby sister.

Excerpt: Pages 10 through 11.

Curriculum Connection: Health

Michael and Mina feed the ill Skellig cod liver oil and Chinese food. Have students use library media center resources to research the health benefits of cod liver oil and create a list of the other nutritional supplements they would give Skellig to help nurse him back to health.

Similar Titles:

Almond, David, ***Counting Stars.*** Random House, 2002, 224pp. $18.99. ISBN: 0385900341. Bantam Doubleday Dell, 2003, 205pp. $5.99. ISBN: 0440418267.
Almond, David, ***The Fire Eaters.*** Random House, 2004, 224pp. $15.95. ISBN: 0385731701. Random House Audio, 2004. $25.00. ISBN: 1400085632.
Almond, David, ***Heaven Eyes.*** Random House, 2001, 240pp. $15.99. ISBN: 0385327706. Random House, 2002, 256pp. $5.50. ISBN: 0440229103. Random House Audio, 2004. $30.00. ISBN: 0807288799.
Almond, David, ***Secret Heart.*** Random House, 2004, 224pp. $5.99. ISBN: 0440418275. Random House Audio, 2004. $30.00. ISBN: 0807209465.
Lowry, Lois, ***Silent Boy.*** Houghton Mifflin, 2003, 192 pp. $15.00. ISBN: 0618282319. Random House, 2005, 208pp. $5.99. ISBN: 0440419808. Random House Audio, 2004. $30.00. ISBN: 0807216925. Random House Audio, 2004. $30.00. CD. ISBN: 0807217662.

3 Bell, Hilari, *The Goblin Wood.*

HarperCollins, 2003, 294pp. $17.89. ISBN: 0060513721. HarperCollins, 2004, 384pp. $6.99. ISBN: 006051373X.

Web Site: <www.sfwa.org/members/bell>
Subjects: Friendship, Goblins, Grieving, Knights and Knighthood, Magic, Prejudices, Witchcraft
Genre: Fantasy
Lists: 2004 BBYA
Levels: BL 6-10, PW 5 up, SLJ 5-8

Annotation: When villagers kill her mother because she is a hedgewitch, 12-year-old Makenna escapes into the woods and is befriended by the Goblins. Five years later Makenna helps save the Goblins from the Hierarchy, which is ridding the land of all magical creatures, and uses her powers to attempt to save the Goblin Wood from the encroaching humans.

Booktalk: Makenna didn't have a choice – she had to set a trap. It was either that or stay awake so they couldn't steal her food and gear. She was sure she heard snickering in the bushes when their thievery got the best of her and she stomped her foot in frustration, right on a sharp stone. They snickered while she hopped around in pain. So Makenna set a trap and lay there in the dark. Then she heard the creature get caught. She snatched it just as it broke free from the snare. It was scarecrow thin, about two and half feet tall, with a long narrow face and sharp teeth. But what caught Makenna's attention wasn't so much his angry eyes, but the rapid beat of his heart. He was a trapped creature and she couldn't bear it. She let him go. You would have thought his release would make him happy, but not this creature! He jumped up and down and started to scream at her. You see, Makenna didn't know that if you free a goblin it is then indebted to you. And from then on, although Cogswhallop was seldom seen, he was always there to warn Makenna if trouble was ahead. Makenna wouldn't realize, until much later, that Cogswhallop and the rest of the Goblins in the Wood would become her family.

Excerpt: From the break on page 37 to the end of first full paragraph on page 41.

Curriculum Connection: Social Studies

The Goblins lived for many years in peace on their side of the Wall. But when the humans were forced to move they planned to take the Wood from the Goblins. Have students use library media center resources to research and discuss countries/regions where this has happened, or is still happening, with one group trying to force another out of an area that they have lived in for generations.

Similar Titles:

Bell, Hilari, ***A Matter of Profit.*** HarperCollins, 2001, 228pp. $17.89. ISBN: 0060295147. HarperCollins, 2003, 368pp. $6.99. ISBN: 0064473007.
Dunkle, Clare B., ***Close Kin.*** The Hollow Kingdom Trilogy. Holt, 2004, 224pp. $16.95. ISBN: 080507497X.
Dunkle, Clare B., ***The Hollow Kingdom.*** The Hollow Kingdom Trilogy. Holt, 2003, 240pp. $16.95. ISBN: 0805073906.
Stroud, Jonathan, ***The Amulet of Samarkand.*** The Bartimaeus Trilogy. Hyperion, 2003, 464pp. $17.95. ISBN: 078681859X. Miramax, 2004, 480pp. $7.99. ISBN: 0786852550. Random House Audio, 2003. $35.00. ISBN: 0807219533.
Stroud, Jonathan, ***The Golem's Eye.*** The Bartimaeus Trilogy. Miramax, 2004, 574pp. $17.95. ISBN: 0786818603. Random House Audio, 2004. $39.95. ISBN: 0807219789.

4 Bell, Hilari, *The Wizard Test.*

HarperCollins, 2005, 166pp. $16.89. ISBN: 0060599413.

Web Site: <www.sfwa.org/members/bell>
Subjects: Friendship, Grieving, Magic, Mothers and Sons, Occupations, Prejudices, Self-Identity, War, Wizards
Genre: Fantasy
Levels: K 6-8

Annotation: Fourteen-year-old Dayven passes the Wizard Test but wants nothing to do with wizardry; he wants to be a Guardian. But the landowner has asked Dayven to spy on the wizards. Dayven learns the true and wonderful nature of being a wizard who can heal and the folly of the war between the Tharn and the Cezan.

Booktalk: Dayven often heard the whisper of "wizard born" and it always sent him into a rage. A rage based on fear and embarrassment. They all knew about his grandmother's disgrace. He was willing to fight any of the Watcherlads who dared to call him "wizard born." Ever since his grandmother, a powerful wizard, had shamed his family, Dayven prayed he would have no magical powers. He *couldn't* be a wizard – he promised his mother on her deathbed that he would have nothing to do with the wizards. He *had* to keep his promise – she died rather than allow a wizard to heal her. Soon Dayven would find out if he inherited his grandmother's wizard's blood. His fourteenth birthday was approaching and he would be summoned to the wizards' tower to endure the Wizard's Test. Every Tharn, at some point during their 14th year, had to take the Wizard's Test, and it was now Dayven's turn.

Excerpt: Third paragraph on page 2 to the first paragraph on page 5.

Curriculum Connections: Science
When the Tharn conquered the Cezan and took over the valley they did not employ the crop rotation methods that the Cezan used and their crops were failing. Based on the information in the book and what they learned during their library media center research on how crops and their rotation affects the soil, have students work in small groups to design a five-year plan of crops and the rotation that would help rebuild the valley's soil for farming.

Similar Titles:
Duane, Diane, *So You Want to Be a Wizard.* The Young Wizards Series. Harcourt, 2003, 336pp. $16.95. ISBN: 0152047387. Harcourt, 2001, 400pp. $6.95. ISBN: 015216250X. Recorded Books, 1998. $44.00. ISBN: 0788720791. Recorded Books, 2000. $69.00. CD. ISBN: 0788749684.
Le Guin, Ursula K., *A Wizard of Earthsea.* Bantam, 2004, 182pp. $14.00. ISBN: 0553383043. Bantam, 1984, 183pp. $7.99. ISBN: 0553262505. Recorded Books, 1992. $42.00. ISBN: 1556907451. Audio Literature, 2003. $35.00. CD. ISBN: 1574535587.

McKillip, Patricia A., ***The Forgotten Beasts of Eld.*** Harcourt, 1996, 343pp. $6.95. ISBN: 0152008691.

Pierce, Tamora, ***Street Magic.*** The Circle Opens Series. Scholastic, 2001, 288pp. $16.95. ISBN: 0590396285. Scholastic, 2002, 312pp. $4.99. ISBN: 0590396439.

Wrede, Patricia C., ***Dealing with Dragons.*** The Enchanted Forest Chronicles. Harcourt, 1990, 224pp. $17.00. ISBN: 0152229000. Harcourt, 2002, 240pp. $5.95. ISBN: 015204566X. Random House Audio, 2001. $27.00. ISBN: 0807261904.

Bruchac, Joseph, *Sacajawea: The Story of Bird Woman and the Lewis and Clark Expedition.*

Harcourt, 2000, 199pp. $17.00. ISBN: 0152022341. Scholastic, 2001, 208pp. $4.99. ISBN: 0439280680. Audio Bookshelf, 2003. $34.95. ISBN: 1883332885. Audio Bookshelf, 2003. $44.95. CD. ISBN: 188333294X.

Web Site: <www.josephbruchac.com>
Subjects: Folklore, Frontier and Pioneer Life, Journeys, Mothers and Sons, Native Americans, Race Relations
Genre: Historical, Multicultural
Levels: K 7-9, PW 7 up, SLJ 7 up, V 7-12

Annotation: Alternating narratives of the Lewis and Clark Expedition from the perspectives of Sacajawea and William Clark, who later helped raise her son, Pomp, are prefaced by Native-American folk tales and Clark's actual journal entries.

Booktalk: Have you and one of your friends ever been telling someone else about something you both saw or did together and your versions didn't sound very much alike? Was one of you lying? Not necessarily. Retellings that differ are pretty normal, since we each see a situation from our own point of view. Now consider the difference between the male and female perspective of a situation, which often further changes the retelling of the events. Let's add a bit more spice to the mix. What if the points of view are of a Native-American woman and a stuffy old white guy? In this particular book the perceptions and retellings are those of Sacajawea and William Clark, two very famous members of the Lewis and Clark Expedition. History doesn't have to be boring and the stories they tell Sacajawea's son, Pomp, about their journey certainly aren't. Makes you wonder if Sacajawea and Clark were really on the same expedition.

Excerpt: Page 3, after the italicized section, to end of page 7.

Curriculum Connection: Social Studies
Have students use library media center resources to research Sacajawea's life *after* she returned from the expedition with Lewis and Clark, as well as what happened to her son, Pomp.

Similar Titles:
O'Dell, Scott, ***Streams to the River, River to the Sea: A Novel of Sacajawea.*** Houghton Mifflin, 1986, 208pp. $16.00. ISBN: 0395404304. Ballantine, 1987, 163pp. $5.99. ISBN: 0449702448.
Roop, Peter, ***Sacagawea: Girl of the Shining Mountains***. Hyperion, 2003, 192pp. $5.99. ISBN: 0786813237.
Schmidt, Thomas and Jeremy Schmidt, ***Saga of Lewis and Clark: Into the Uncharted West.*** DK Publishing, 2001, 210pp. $25.00. ISBN: 078948076X.
Smith Roland, ***The Captain's Dog: My Journey with the Lewis and Clark Tribe.*** Harcourt, 1999, 296pp. $17.00. ISBN: 0152019898. Harcourt, 2000, 304pp. $6.00. ISBN: 0152026967.
White, Alana J., ***Sacagawea: Westward with Lewis and Clark.*** Native American Biographies. Enslow, 1997, 128pp. $19.95. ISBN: 0894908677.

6. Carman, Patrick, *The Dark Hills Divide.*

The Land of Elyon Series. Orchard, 2005, 272pp. $11.95. ISBN: 0439700930. Brilliance Audio, 2005. $24.95. ISBN: 1597373915. Brilliance Audio, 2005. $26.95. CD. ISBN: 1597373931.

Web Site: <www.patrickcarman.com>
Subjects: Animals, Cats, Crime, Fathers and Daughters, Journeys, Magic
Genre: Fantasy
Levels: K 5-7

Annotation: Feisty and inquisitive 12-year-old Alexa Daley, the daughter of the Mayor of Lathbury, one of the four walled cities of Elyon, discovers a hidden door that leads outside the wall. Talking animals help her thwart a takeover of the cities by the criminals who were forced to build the cities' walls many years before.

Booktalk: You would think spending the summer holed up in a musty dusty old library would be boring – right? Wrong! What if in that library there were secrets to be discovered, both in the books and in the medallions that hang around the necks of the library cats? Alexa, the Mayor's daughter, has always wanted to know what's on the other side of the 45-foot high walls that surround the cities of Elyon. Even the roads between the cities are walled in. Alexa wants to explore beyond the walls. She wants to know what howls out there at night. At least she thinks she does. Everyone knows that Alexa skulks around the walls of Bridewell every summer, looking for a way out. But this summer is different – Warvold, the leader of Elyon, has died and Alexa was with him when it happened. She didn't tell anyone she took the tiny silver key from around his neck. Alexa is sure she can find the door the silver key will open and she knows the best place to start is in the library. She is positive the key is to a door that leads to the other side of the wall and to a fascinating new world. If Alexa only knew what she was about to encounter, she may have left the key around the dead Warvold's neck.

Actually, no – knowing Alexa she would have went headlong into the adventure anyway!

Excerpt: Page 12, fourth paragraph, through page 16.

Curriculum Connections: Language Arts, Science

Alexa is able to talk to the animals because of the magic stone she finds in the pool. Have students use library media center resources to research an animal they would like to have a conversation with if they found such a stone. Have them write the dialogue they think might happen during their first conversation, basing it on what they have learned about this animal's behaviors, habitat, what it likes to eat, and the other types of animals with which it interacts.

Similar Titles:

Coville, Bruce, ***Into the Land of the Unicorns.*** The Unicorn Chronicles. Scholastic, 1999, 159pp. $4.50. ISBN: 0439108381. Random House Audio, 1998. $29.00. ISBN: 0807279633.

DuPrau, Jeanne, ***The People of Sparks.*** Random House, 2004, 352pp. $15.95. ISBN: 0375828249. Random House, 2005, 352pp. $5.99. ISBN: 0375828257. Random House Audio, 2004. $36.00. ISBN: 140008489X. Random House Audio, 2004. $50.00. CD. ISBN: 1400089905.

Ende, Michael, ***The Neverending Story.*** Penguin, 1997, 396 pp. $22.99. ISBN: 0525457585. Penguin, 1984, 384pp. $13.00. ISBN: 0140074317. Penguin, 1993, 448pp. $7.99. ISBN: 0140386335.

Ende, Michael, ***The Night of Wishes.*** Farrar, Straus & Giroux, 1995, 224pp. $7.95. ISBN: 0374455031.

Jacques, Brian, ***Redwall.*** The Redwall Series. Philomel, 1987, 351pp. $23.99. ISBN: 0399214240. Penguin, 2000, 352pp. $7.99. ISBN: 0142302376. Random House Audio, 2000. $35.00. ISBN: 0807281905. Random House Audio, 2001. $49.95. CD. ISBN: 0807262048.

Cassidy, Cathy, *Dizzy.*

Viking, 2004, 256pp. $15.99. ISBN: 0670059366.

Web Site: <www.cathycassidy.com>
Subjects: Child Neglect, Drugs, Fires, Kidnapping, Mothers and Daughters, Self-Identity
Genres: International, Realistic
Levels: BL 7-9, K 5-7, PW 5 up, SLJ 5-8

Annotation: Twelve-year-old Dizzy willingly goes with the hippie mother she hasn't seen in eight years, but finds she doesn't like her mother's lifestyle of living in teepees at outdoor festivals in Scotland, or the way her mother and boyfriend neglect their children.

Booktalk: Dizzy has dreamt of the day her mother would return. She impatiently waits for her birthday each year, watching for the mailman and praying he will bring her something from her mother. Her mother is a wandering hippie who couldn't handle settling down and raising a family. And here it is, her 12th birthday and the present she gets is unbelievable – her mother is sitting on the couch in their living room. At first Dizzy doesn't recognize her, but she knows she has to be her mother. The mother she hasn't seen in years now wants to take Dizzy with her to the Solstice Festival in Scotland, but Dizzy can sense her dad does not like this idea at all. That's why she is very surprised when Storm (she doesn't want to be called Mom – it makes her feel old, and well, like a mother!) wakes Dizzy up early the next morning and says they need to get on the road. When Dizzy tries to say goodbye to her dad he barely wakes up enough to acknowledge her because he thinks she is off to school for the day. If only he, and Dizzy, knew what Storm was up to.

Excerpt: First paragraph on page 12 through page 13.

Curriculum Connection: Social Studies
The festivals celebrated around the world, such as the Solstice Festival, are based on old religions, such as those of the Celts and Greeks. Have students use library media center resources to research the various festivals that relate to the seasons and the calendar. Have them describe the type of activities and crafts they might see at these festivals.

Similar Titles:

Breuilly, Elizabeth, **Religions of the World: The Illustrated Guide to Origins, Beliefs, Traditions and Festivals.** Facts on File, 1997, 160pp. $29.95. ISBN: 081603723X.
Danziger, Paula, **There's a Bat in Bunk Five.** Putnam, 1998, 154pp. $4.99. ISBN: 0698116895. Random House Audio, 1985. $15.98. ISBN: 0807218286.
Hunter, Molly, **The Walking Stones.** Harcourt, 1996, 168pp. $5.00. ISBN: 0152009957.
Krisher, Trudy B., **Kinship.** Doubleday, 1997, 340pp. $15.95. ISBN: 0385446950. Recorded Books, 2003. $54.00. ISBN: 0788790250.
Young, Ella, **Celtic Wonder Tales.** Dover, 1996, 224pp. $7.95. ISBN: 048628896X.

Clark, Clara Gillow, *Hill Hawk Hattie.*

Candlewick, 2003, 159pp. $15.99. ISBN: 0763619639. Candlewick, 2004, 176pp. $5.99. ISBN: 0763625590.

Subjects: Fathers and Daughters, Frontier and Pioneer Life, Grieving, Occupations, Self-Esteem
Genre: Historical
Levels: BL 4-7, SLJ 4-7, V 6-9

Annotation: Eleven-year-old Hattie is grieving over the recent death of her mother in their remote 1800's New England cabin when her father decides to dress her as a boy and take her on a logging trip down the Delaware.

Booktalk: Hattie wasn't much of a cook, that's for sure. Her biscuits were as heavy as lead balls and she burned most everything she tried to cook or bake. She knew her father missed her mother's cooking almost as much as he missed her, but Hattie just hadn't gotten the knack of cooking and baking down before her mother died. Now all she tried to do is to stay out of her father's way so she didn't get a slap across the head. He'd always been a gruff man, but since Hattie's mother gave up on living he was more than gruff, he was downright mean. But, Hattie couldn't have expected what he gave her as a birthday present. She wanted a dress and some ribbons for her hair, but he bought her boy clothes. Boy clothes and a hat to cover up her hair. Hattie's father had decided it was time Hattie become his son instead of his daughter. It was time she learned how to do men's work. Maybe he thinks she will be better in the woods than she is in the kitchen. Will Hattie prove him right or wrong?

Excerpt: First paragraph on page 10 to italicized text on page 12.

Curriculum Connection: Social Studies
This story is set in the 1800s when New England was still rich with timber. Have students use library media center resources to research the timber industry during this time period and discuss how the logs were transported to the mills.

Similar Titles:
Avi, ***The True Confessions of Charlotte Doyle.*** Orchard, 2003, 224pp. $9.95. ISBN: 0439327318. HarperCollins, 2004, 204pp. $2.99. ISBN: 0060739479.
Clark, Clara Gillow, ***Hattie on Her Way.*** Candlewick, 2005, 208pp. $15.99. ISBN: 0763622869.
Crew, Linda, ***Fire on the Wind.*** Random House, 1995, 208pp. $12.00. ISBN: 0375895124.
Hahn, Mary Downing, ***The Gentleman Outlaw and Me–Eli.*** Houghton Mifflin, 1996, 224pp. $16.00. ISBN: 039573083X. HarperTrophy, 1997, 192pp. $4.99. ISBN: 0380728834.
Rinaldi, Ann, ***Girl in Blue.*** Scholastic, 2001, 272pp. $15.95. ISBN: 0439073367. Scholastic, 2005, 320pp. $5.99. ISBN: 0439676460.

9 Clinton, Cathryn, *A Stone in My Hand.*

Candlewick, 2002, 208pp. $15.99. ISBN: 0763613886. Candlewick, 2004, 192pp. $5.99. ISBN: 0763625612.

Web Site: <www.catherineclinton.com>
Subjects: Brothers and Sisters, Family Problems, Race Relations, Religion, Violence
Genres: International, Multicultural, Realistic
Levels: BL 6-12, K 6 up, PW 6 up, SLJ 5-8, V 6-9

Annotation: Eleven-year-old Malaak fears her missing father is dead and that her rebellious older brother will get in trouble as their family is caught up in the violence between the Jews and Palestinians in Gaza.

Booktalk: Every day Malaak climbs the stairs to the roof and watches for her father. Her eyes linger on the very spot where he stood and waved goodbye to her before he left their Palestinian neighborhood in Gaza City to find work in Israel. Malaak prays that her brother, now even more rebellious with their father gone, will not join the Islamic Jihad. Malaak wishes Adbo, her tame dove, could fly all the way to Israel to bring her father back, but she doesn't know if her father even made it out of the city alive. As she stands alone on the roof, day after day, waiting and watching, the violence in Gaza City and their neighborhood escalates. Malaak's fear of losing yet another family member also increases as she helplessly watches her brother becoming bolder and bolder in his Jihad involvement. Will she lose her only brother as well?

Excerpt: Page 28 to page 30, end of second paragraph.

Curriculum Connection: Social Studies
Have students visit the library media center to examine atlases and other maps to locate the Gaza Strip. Using the maps and information they found in other library media center resources, such as up-to-date Internet sources of population statistics, have students discuss the size of the Gaza Strip, the number of people who live there, as well as how Malaak's neighborhood is similar or different from their own.

Similar Titles:
Al-Windawi, Thura, ***Thura's Diary: My Life in Wartime Iraq.*** Viking, 2004, 131pp. $15.99. ISBN: 0670058866.
Armstrong, Jennifer, ***Shattered: Stories of Children and War.*** Knopf, 2002, 176pp. $15.95. ISBN: 0375811125. Bantam Doubleday Dell, 2003, 176pp. $5.99. ISBN: 0440237653.
Jiang, Ji-Li, ***Red Scarf Girl: A Memoir of the Cultural Revolution.*** HarperCollins, 1997, 285pp. $16.99. ISBN: 0060275855. HarperCollins, 1998, 285pp. $6.99. ISBN: 0064462080. Recorded Books, 1999. $59.20. ISBN: 0788730053.

Miklowitz, Gloria D., ***The Enemy Has a Face.*** Erdmans, 2004, 143pp. $8.00. ISBN: 0802852610.

Naidoo, Beverley, ***Out of Bounds: Seven Stories of Conflict and Hope.*** HarperCollins, 2003, 192pp. $17.89. ISBN: 0060508000.

Cofer, Judith Ortiz, *Call Me Maria.*

First Person Fiction Series. Orchard, 2004, 127pp. $16.95. ISBN: 0439385776.

Web Site: <www.english.uga.edu/~jcofer/home.html>
Subjects: Divorce, Fathers and Daughters, Moving, Puerto Rican Americans, Race Relations, Writing
Genres: Multicultural, Realistic
Levels: BL 6-9, K 7 up, SLJ 5-8

Annotation: Fifteen-year-old Maria narrates her move from Puerto Rico to New York City with her father when he returns to the barrio that he calls home, while her mother remains in Puerto Rico. Told via letters, poetry, and prose.

Booktalk: How many languages do you speak? One? Two? How many of you speak three? Maria grew up in Puerto Rico speaking both Spanish and English because her mother is an English language teacher. Life was pleasant on the island until Maria's father couldn't stand living there any more. He didn't like the way he was made fun of for the way he speaks Spanish. He didn't want to be an outsider anymore. He wanted to go home to the New York City neighborhood where he grew up. Maria's mother would have nothing to do with leaving her beloved island. So, Maria is forced to choose – between staying in Puerto Rico with her mother and starting a new life in New York with her father. It was a very difficult decision, but she chooses to begin a new life with her father. Learning to live in a tiny apartment in a big city isn't easy for Maria, but she knows she will have more opportunities here. And it is in this multiethnic environment that Maria learns her third language – Spanglish, a combination of English and Spanish that everyone in the barrio learns to speak, even her new friend, Uma, who is from India.

Excerpt: Pages 25 through 27.

Curriculum Connections: Foreign Languages, Language Arts
Have students explore the English/Spanish, English/French, and other foreign language dictionaries in the library media center to prepare for a discussion about the variety of languages that are spoken in the daily conversations we have. Address the different languages from which commonly used terms are derived, as well as phrases that are a mixture of languages. Have students share bilingual phrases that are used in their own homes.

Similar Titles:
Cofer, Judith Ortiz, ***The Meaning of Consuelo.*** Farrar, Straus & Giroux, 2003, 200pp. $20.00. ISBN: 0374205094.
Cofer, Judith Ortiz, ***Silent Dancing: A Partial Remembrance of a Puerto Rican Childhood.*** Arte Publico Press, 1990, 168pp. $12.95. ISBN: 1558850155.
Miller-Lachmann, Lyn, ***Once Upon a Cuento.*** Curbstone Press, 2003, 228pp. $15.95. ISBN: 1880684993.
Mohr, Nicholasa, ***Going Home.*** Penguin, 1999, 192pp. $5.99. ISBN: 0141306440.
Polikoff, Barbara Garland, ***Why Does the Coqui Sing?*** Holiday House, 2004, 228pp. $16.95. ISBN: 0823418170.

11 Cohn, Rachel, *The Steps.*

Simon & Schuster, 2003, 137pp. $15.95. ISBN: 0689845499. Simon & Schuster, 2004, 144pp. $5.99. ISBN: 0689874146. Random House Audio, 2003. $18.00. ISBN: 0807215589.

Web Site: <www.rachelcohn.com>
Subjects: Divorce, Fathers and Daughters, Grandmothers, Stepfamilies
Genres: Humor, International, Realistic
Lists: 2004 CN
Levels: BL 4-7, K 6-9, PW 8-12, SLJ 5-8

Annotation: Twelve-year-old Annabel visits her father in Australia where he lives with his new wife, baby, and stepchildren. She intends to convince him to move back home to New York City with her and her mother, but then Annabel learns that her mother is pregnant and getting married to one of her least favorite classmate's father.

Booktalk: Steps are to walk on – right? Well, these steps I want to stomp on! They aren't inanimate objects – they are my step siblings who live in Australia. Can you believe my dad left Manhattan, my mom, and me to go live in Australia, land of kangaroos? Not only did he leave us, he up and marries some woman with kids so they get to see him every day and I don't. This woman he married must be really weird. Who in their right mind names a kid after a cow anyway? What kid wants to have the name Angus! And you know what – it gets worse. They now have a baby of their own. My dad actually had another kid with another woman. How gross is that? Now I have to spend time in their house and try to be nice to these Australians. There is no way I am considering them family. But, at least by being over there I can convince my dad that he really needs to stop this nonsense and come home. And, I am NOT going to become friends with this Lucy chick. I don't care that she is my age. I am NOT going to make this easy on my dad. And, I am NOT going to have fun in Australia! What a way to have to spend Christmas. Give me a break!

Excerpt: Chapter One.

Curriculum Connection: Language Arts, Social Studies

Annabel does not like the way Australians abbreviate words such as "brekkie" for breakfast and "noodies" for noodles. Have students use library media center resources to research and discuss how different cultural groups change the basic spelling and pronunciation of words that are common to the English language. Have students work together to develop a list of abbreviated terms that are used by their families.

Similar Titles:

Block, Joel D., ***Stepliving for Teens: Getting Along with Stepparents and Siblings.*** Penguin, 2001, 144pp. $4.99. ISBN: 0843175680.

Bryant, Ann, ***One Mom Too Many.*** The Step-Chain Series. Lobster Press, 2004, 190pp. $3.95. ISBN: 1894222784.

Friesen, Gayle, ***Losing Forever.*** Kids Can Press, 2003, 247pp. $16.95. ISBN: 1553370317. Kids Can Press, 2003, 248pp. $6.95. ISBN: 1553370325.

Hurwitz, Jane, ***Coping in a Blended Family.*** The Coping Series. Rosen, 1997, 102pp. $26.50. ISBN: 0823920771.

Worthen, Tom and Kyle Hernandez, ***Broken Hearts...Healing: Young Poets Speak Out on Divorce.*** Poet Tree Press, 2001, 248pp. $26.95. ISBN: 1588761509. Poet Tree Press, 2001, 248pp. $14.95. ISBN: 1588761517.

Cooper, Ilene, *Sam I Am.*

Scholastic, 2004, 252pp. $15.95. ISBN: 0439439671.

Web Site: <www.ilenecooper.com>
Subjects: Brothers and Sisters, Grandmothers, Holidays, Jewish Americans, Prejudices, Religion, Schools, World War II
Genres: Multicultural, Realistic
Levels: K 4-7, PW 4-7, SLJ 5-7

Annotation: Twelve-year-old Sam, whose father is Jewish and mother is Christian, questions God's existence as his family struggles with how to celebrate Christmas and Hanukkah. A school assignment on the Holocaust helps him better understand his Jewish heritage.

Booktalk: It wasn't my fault, but Mom looked at me like it was. Pluto is the one who knocked over the Hanukkah Bush. But because I was the only one, only human, in the family room when it happened Mom blamed it on me. Now she is in the kitchen, holding a tiny glass angel with one wing broken off that she has had since she was a child. She's in there crying over the broken ornaments and we are pretending we don't know she's crying. We all know it was a Christmas tree, but you see my dad is Jewish and he wasn't too keen on the idea of a Christmas tree, so they kind of compromised and the Hanukkah Bush name stuck. Now mom says we aren't going to put up a new tree. She says it just wouldn't be the same. This is going to be the worst Christmas ever. Where am I supposed to put the Christmas presents? I can't very well put them under the shiny new Menorah that has suddenly appeared on the mantle. And can you believe Mom has invited both grandmothers over for a Christmas Eve/Hanukkah dinner? They can't handle being the same room together for five minutes without getting into a fight. They hate each other and I hate what is happening to our Christmas! Why couldn't we have gone somewhere on vacation or done anything else instead of this combined Christmas and Hannukkah celebration?

Excerpt: Page 37 through first paragraph on page 40.

Curriculum Connection: Social Studies

The Holocaust unit at school disturbed Sam, especially when he realizes that even the great-grandchildren of Jews were executed. Have students use library media center resources to research and discuss first person accounts of people who were children during the Holocaust and how they survived.

Similar Titles:

Benderly, Beryl Lieff, ***Jason's Miracle: A Hanukkah Story.*** Albert Whitman, 2000, 120pp. $14.95. ISBN: 0807537810. DIANE Publishing, 2004, 114pp. $15.00. ISBN: 0756777925.

Feinstein, Edward, ***Tough Questions Jews Ask: A Young Adult's Guide To Building a Jewish Life.*** Jewish Lights Publishing, 2003, 160pp. $14.95. ISBN: 158023139X. Jewish Lights Publishing, 2004, 72pp. $8.95. ISBN: 158023187X.

Paterson, Katherine, ***A Midnight Clear: Family Christmas Stories.*** Penguin, 2000, 212pp. $6.99. ISBN: 0142300373.

Robinson, Barbara, ***The Best Christmas Pageant Ever.*** HarperCollins, 1972, 96pp. $16.89. ISBN: 0060250445. HarperTrophy, 1998, 96pp. $5.50. ISBN: 006447044X. Recorded Books, 2000. $19.00. CD. ISBN: 0788737368.

Rosen, Michael, ***Elijah's Angel: A Story for Chanukah and Christmas.*** Harcourt, 1997, 32pp. $7.00. ISBN 0152015582.

Couloumbis, Audrey, *Getting Near To Baby.*

Putnam, 1999, 211pp. $17.99. ISBN: 039923389X. Putnam, 2001, 224pp. $5.99. ISBN: 0698118928. Random House Audio, 2001. $22.00. ISBN: 0807261955.

Web Site: <www.audreycouloumbis.com>
Subjects: Death, Family Problems, Grieving, Infants, Sisters
Genres: Realistic
Awards: 2000 Newbery Honor
Lists: 2000 CN
Levels: K 6-8, LJ 6-8, PW 5 up, SLJ 6-8, V 6-9

Annotation: After their baby sister dies, thirteen-year-old Willa Jo and eight-year-old Little Sister are sent to live with their aunt. Missing their mother and grieving for Baby Sister, Willa Jo seeks early morning solace on the roof and when Little Sister, who hasn't spoken since the baby died, joins her they begin to come to terms with their grief.

Booktalk: Did you ever wonder how you are supposed to act when something terrible happens to your family? Do you become silent like Little Sister in *Getting Near to Baby* or do you get a bit on the ornery side like her older sister Willa Jo? When Baby Sister dies the two sisters are sent to live with Aunt Patty and Uncle Hob. Aunt Patty has always been able to fix any problem, so she sets about "fixin" their grief by buying them new clothes and sending them off to Bible camp. But Willa Jo has other ideas and becomes friends with the unruly and unconventional neighbor kids, much to prissy Aunt Patty's dismay. One morning Willa Jo finds herself sitting on the roof, waiting for the sun to rise. She isn't quite sure why she's there, but she knows it feels right and she doesn't mind at all when Little Sister joins her. Little Sister hasn't said a word since Baby Sister died from bad drinking water. Neither girl knew Little Sister would speak that morning, but her words made all kinds of sense and began to heal their hearts.

Excerpt: Chapter 1.

Curriculum Connection: Language Arts
Share with students various poetry collections from the library media center, highlighting different types of poetry. Ask them to select a poem they like and write their own poem, in that style, about Willa Jo and Little Sister and how they dealt with their grief.

Similar Titles:
DiCamillo, Kate, *Tiger Rising.* Candlewick, 2001, 128pp. $15.99. ISBN: 0763609110. Candlewick, 2002, 128pp. $5.99. ISBN: 0763618985. Listening Library, 2004. $23.00. ISBN: 0807288705.

McDaniel, Lurlene, ***The Girl Death Left Behind.*** Bantam Doubleday Dell, 1999, 176pp. $4.99. ISBN: 0553570919.

O'Dell, Scott, ***Island of the Blue Dolphins.*** Houghton Mifflin, 1960, 192pp. $16.00. ISBN: 0395069629. Yearling, 1971, 192pp. $6.50. ISBN: 0440439884. Random House Audio, 2004. $36.00. ISBN: 0807283266. Random House Audio, 2004. $35.00. CD. ISBN: 0807217794.

Paterson, Katherine, ***Bridge to Terabithia.*** HarperCollins, 1977, 144pp. $15.99. ISBN: 0690013590. HarperTrophy, 2005, 208pp. $5.99. ISBN: 0060734019. HarperChildrensAudio, 2005. $25.95. ISBN: 0060758333.

Shearer, Alex, ***The Great Blue Yonder.*** Houghton Mifflin, 2002, 192pp. $15.00. ISBN: 0618212574. Scholastic, 2004, 192pp. $4.99. ISBN: 0439561272. BBC Audio Books America, 2003. $32.95. ISBN: 0754063550.

14

Creech, Sharon, *Granny Torrelli Makes Soup.*

HarperCollins, 2003, 141pp. $16.89. ISBN: 00602929011. HarperCollins, 2005, 160pp. 5.99. ISBN: 0064409600. HarperCollinsAudio, 2003. $18.00. ISBN: 0060564326.

Web Site: <www.sharoncreech.com>
Subjects: Cooking, Disabilities, Friendship, Grandmothers
Genres: Multicultural, Realistic
Lists: 2004 CN
Levels: BL 4-6, PW 3-7, SLJ 4-7

Annotation: Twelve-year-old Rosie doesn't always get along with her best friend, Bailey, who is blind. Granny Torrelli cooks with them and tells tales of her youth to help them understand their jealous feelings when a new kid moves into the neighborhood and changes their friendship.

Booktalk: You'd have thought he would be proud of me. I spent hours learning how to read like he does. It isn't easy you know, not like when all you have to do is look at the words. I learned how to read with my fingertips. I wanted to show Bailey that I cared enough about him to learn how to read like he does. But do you think he was happy when I showed him what I could do? No! He was absolutely furious with me. He actually slammed the door in my face. He didn't want to talk to me anymore. Well, that Bailey can just sit over in his house all by himself for all I care. Who cares that we have been friends since we were little kids? Who cares that I walked around with tissue paper over my face so I could see the world like he did back when we were little? I'll show that Bailey. I just won't have anything to do with him. Granny Torrelli seems to think making soup will help. Fine! Let's make some soup! But, I am NOT sharing any with Bailey. Well, maybe....

Excerpt: Pages 16 through 22.

Curriculum Connection: Health

When Bailey was very young he saw shapes and shadows, but he could not distinguish print so he was not able to learn how to read visually. Have students use library media resources to research childhood blindness and how visually impaired children learn to use Braille to read.

Similar Titles:

Alexander, Sally Hobart, ***Do You Remember the Color Blue?: Questions Children Ask About Being Blind.*** Viking, 2000, 80pp. $16.99. ISBN: 0670880434. Puffin, 2002, 78pp. $7.99. ISBN: 0142300802.

Ayer, Katherine, ***Under Copp's Hill.*** The American Girl History Mysteries. Pleasant Company, 2000, 176pp. $9.95. ISBN: 1584850892. Pleasant Company, 2000, 176pp. $5.95. ISBN: 1584850884.

Bloor, Edward, ***Tangerine.*** Harcourt, 1997, 304pp. $17.00. ISBN: 015201246X. Scholastic, 2001, 294pp. $5.99. ISBN: 0439286034.

Lasky, Kathryn, ***An American Spring: Sofia's Immigrant Diary, The North End of Boston, 1903.*** The My America Series. Scholastic, 2004, 112pp. $12.95. ISBN: 0439370450. Scholastic, 2004, 112pp. $4.99. ISBN: 0439370469.

Peck, Richard, ***A Long Way From Chicago.*** Dial, 1998, 148pp. $15.99. ISBN: 0803722907. Penguin, 2004, 160pp. ISBN: 0142401102. Random House Audio, 2000. $25.00. ISBN: 0807261629. Random House Audio, 2005. $19.95. CD. ISBN: 0307243206.

Creedon, Catherine, *Blue Wolf.*

15

HarperCollins, 2003, 182pp. $15.99. ISBN: 006050868X. HarperCollins, 2005, 192pp. $5.99. ISBN: 0060508701.

Subjects: Animals, Fathers and Sons, Folklore, Grieving, Korean Americans, Magic, Music, Self-Identity, Track and Field, Wolves
Genres: Fantasy, Multicultural, Sports
Levels: BL 4-8, K 5-9, PW 4-7, SLJ 5-8, V 6-9

Annotation: After his mother dies, 14-year-old Jamie is sent to live with a mysterious aunt in her primitive cabin in the Pacific Northwest. He discovers that his Korean father and uncle are able to shape shift into wolf form and that he must learn to play the specific tune on a bone flute that will change his aunt into her wolf form.

Booktalk: Jamie jumped up and down and shook his arms, trying to stay warm before the meet began. It may be June but the rain made it feel like March. He jogged over to his teammates who got quiet when they saw him. Some looked away, unable to meet his eyes. Lots of people acted that way around him since his mother died. He tried to pretend he didn't notice. He concentrated on his event. This was the last race of the season and although he was the fastest distance runner on the team, he had to work harder at the shorter distance races. Jaime got into position and that's when he heard them. He heard their panting, faint but steady. It was the wolves. The first time he heard them he was so frightened he ran so fast to keep ahead of them that he set a state record in the race. Now he anxiously waited for them to run with him and he could even smell their wet fur when it rained, but he never saw them. Nevertheless, Jamie was sure they were real, especially when he felt a sharp nip on his ankle when the starting gun went off.

Excerpt: Page 9 through last full paragraph on page 12.

Curriculum Connections: Language Arts, Social Studies
Jamie's father said that Jamie has the face of a Mongol warrior and told him stories about the Mongol's legendary ancestor, a fierce blue wolf. Have students use library media center resources to research other Asian animal-related legends and orally share the stories they learned with the rest of the class.

Similar Titles:

Barron, T.A., ***The Ancient One.*** Philomel, 1992, 368pp. $19.99. ISBN: 0399218998. Penguin, 2003, 320pp. $6.99. ISBN: 0441010326.

Kindl, Patrice, ***Owl In Love.*** Houghton Mifflin, 1993, 204pp. $16.00. ISBN: 0395661625. Houghton Mifflin, 2004, 224pp. $6.99. ISBN: 0618439102. Recorded Books, 1998. $37.00. ISBN: 0788720783

Na, An, ***Step From Heaven.*** Front Street, 2001, 156pp. $15.95. ISBN: 1886910588. Penguin, 2002, 160pp. $7.99. ISBN: 0142500275. Random House Audio, 2002. $25.00. ISBN: 0807207217. Random House Audio, 2004. $35.00. CD. ISBN: 0807216127.

Park, Linda Sue, ***My Name Was Keoko.*** Houghton Mifflin, 2002, 208pp. $16.00. ISBN: 0618133356. Yearling, 2004, 208pp. $5.99. ISBN: 0440419441. Recorded Books, 2003. $42.00. ISBN: 1402546556.

Thesman, Jean, ***The Other Ones.*** Viking, 1999, 181pp. $15.99. ISBN: 0670885940. Penguin, 2001, 191pp. $5.99. ISBN: 0141312467.

Curtis, Christopher Paul, *Bud, Not Buddy.*

Delacorte, 1999, 243pp. $16.95. ISBN: 0385323069. Random House, 2004, 272pp. $6.50. ISBN: 0553494104. Random House Audio, 2000. $22.00. ISBN: 0553526758. Random House Audio, 2001. $36.00. CD. ISBN: 0807205028.

Web Site: <www.christopherpaulcurtis.com>
Subjects: African Americans, The Depression, Foster Homes, Grandfathers, Grieving, Journeys, Music, Orphans, Runaways, Self-Identity
Genres: Historical, Multicultural
Awards: 2000 Coretta Scott King, 2000 Newbery
Lists: 2000 BBYA, 2000 CN
Levels: BL 4-7, LJ 4-7, PW 4-7, SLJ 4-7

Annotation: After his mother dies, Bud, a 10-year-old African-American orphan, runs away from a foster home, traveling from Flint to Grand Rapids, Michigan in search of the man he thinks is his father, but who proves to be his grandfather. His grandfather is the leader of the 1930's Dusky Devastation of the Depression jazz band, who becomes Bud's new family.

Booktalk: I got Momma's two special rocks in my pocket and the posters of my father in my suitcase – all the important stuff in the world. I'm headed to Grand Rapids, Michigan. It's a long way from Flint, but I can't stand those foster homes no more. Momma died four years ago and they keep putting me with families who really don't want me. Some of them are just downright mean. Being locked in that shed with the bats and spiders made the decision for me. I'm headed out of here. I'll catch a ride or I'll walk the whole way, but I'm going to get to Grand Rapids. That's where my father is. And when I find my father, Mr. Herman E. Calloway, he'll want to keep me. Won't he?

Excerpt: Pages 1 through 6.

Curriculum Connection: Social Studies
Have students use library media center resources to research the Great Depression and how it affected children and teenagers, using as many first person accounts as they can find.

Similar Titles:
Armstrong, William H., **Sounder.** HarperCollins, 1987, 116pp. $16.89. ISBN: 0060201444. HarperCollins, 2001, 96pp. $7.00. ISBN: 0060935480. HarperAudio, 1995. $18.00. ISBN: 1559946717.
Cleary, Beverly, **Dear Mr. Henshaw.** Morrow, 1983, 144pp. $16.89. ISBN: 0688024068. HarperCollins, 2000, 134pp. $5.99. ISBN: 0380709589. Recorded Books, 1992. $19.00. ISBN: 1556905947. Recorded Books, 2000. $19.00. CD. ISBN: 0788737406.

Creech, Sharon, ***Walk Two Moons.*** HarperCollins, 1995, 288pp. $17.89. ISBN: 0060233370. HarperCollins, 2004, 304pp. $6.99. ISBN: 0060560134. Books on Tape, 2000. $30.00. ISBN: 0736650237. Random House Audio, 2004. $40.00. CD. ISBN: 0807220124.

Fleischman, Sid, ***The Whipping Boy.*** Morrow, 1986, 87pp. $16.99. ISBN: 0688062164. HarperCollins, 2003, 86pp. $5.99. ISBN: 0060521228. Recorded Books, 1993. $19.00. ISBN: 1556908571. Recorded Books, 2000. $19.00. CD. ISBN: 0788734571.

Hesse, Karen, ***Out of the Dust.*** Scholastic, 1997, 227pp. $15.95. ISBN: 0590360809. Scholastic, 1999, 176pp. $4.99. ISBN: 0590371258. Listening Library, 1998. $18.00. ISBN: 080728050X.

17 Curtis, Christopher Paul, *The Watsons Go to Birmingham–1963.*

Delacorte, 1995, 210pp. $16.95. ISBN: 0385321759. Bantam Doubleday Dell, 1997, 224pp. $6.50. ISBN: 0440414121. Listening Library, 1996. $26.00. ISBN: 0553477862. Random House Audio, 2004. $34.00. CD. ISBN: 0807217778.

Web Site: <www.christopherpaulcurtis.com>
Subjects: African Americans, Brothers, Emotional Problems, Family Problems, Grandmothers, Journeys, Prejudices, Race Relations
Genres: Historical, Multicultural
Awards: 1996 Coretta Scott King Honor, 1996 Newbery Honor
Lists: 1996 BBYA, 1996 CN, 1997 YAC
Levels: BL 4-8, K 5-7, PW 5 up, SLJ 6 up

Annotation: Ten-year-old Kenny Watson and his family drive from Flint, Michigan to Birmingham, Alabama, where they hope Grandmother can straighten out the wayward older brother Byron. They arrive just as the Civil Rights Movement is heating up and one of the churches is bombed.

Booktalk: No matter how bad things get you need to keep your sense of humor. And things could get very bad for African Americans back in the 1960s. Imagine not being able to go into a restaurant or stay at a motel because of your color. Kenny and the rest of the weird Watson family had a great sense of humor, but everyone's sense of humor was wearing thin with the antics of Kenny's older brother Byron, officially a juvenile delinquent as far as the Watsons are concerned. For example, Bryon was so stuck on himself he kissed his reflection in the mirror of the car. He should have known better than to put warm lips on a freezing cold mirror in the dead of winter. That's why he's now referred to as the Lipless Wonder. As entertaining as Byron's antics could be it was time to get him straightened out and if anyone could do it, it was Grandma in Birmingham, Alabama. But what happens in Birmingham is no laughing matter.

Excerpt: Page 1 through the last paragraph on page 5.

Curriculum Connection: Social Studies
The church bombing while the Watsons were in Birmingham actually occurred. Have students read the epilogue, use library media center resources to research the actual event, and discuss what they learned about the Civil Rights Movement and how it impacted the world as we know it today.

Similar Titles:
Armistead, John, *The Return of Gabriel.* Milkweed, 2002, 218pp. $17.95. ISBN: 157131637X. Milkweed, 2002, 240pp. $6.95. ISBN: 1571316388.
Beals, Melba Patillo, *Warriors Don't Cry.* Simon & Schuster, 1994, 240pp. $5.99. ISBN: 0671899007. Simon & Schuster, 1995, 336pp. $14.00. ISBN: 0671866397.
Davis, Ossie, *Just Like Martin.* Penguin, 1995, 215pp. $5.99. ISBN: 0140370951.
Morrison, Toni, *Remember: The Journey to School Integration.* Houghton Mifflin, 2004, 80pp. $18.00. ISBN: 061839740X.
Murphy, Rita, *Black Angels.* Random House, 2002, 163pp. $4.99. ISBN: 0440229340. Recorded Books, 2001. $28.00. ISBN: 0788789724.

D'Adamo, Francesco, *Iqbal.*

Atheneum, 2003, 122pp. $15.95. ISBN: 0689854455. Simon & Schuster, 2005, 128pp. $4.99. ISBN: 1416903291.

Subjects: Child Abuse, Murder, Occupations, Self-Identity, Survival
Genres: International, Multicultural, Realistic
Lists: 2004 CN, 2004 TC
Levels: BL 4-7, K 5-9, PW 5-7, SLJ 4-7

Annotation: A girl in bondage to the same owner narrates a fictional account of the life of Iqbal Masih, a 13-year-old Pakistani who was murdered after he escaped from bondage in a carpet factory and garnered world interest in the liberation of child workers.

Booktalk: How many of you do or would like to have a job and some extra spending money? But, what if the money you made was then taken right back from you to pay for your daily living expenses – food, room and board, and other basic necessities? Your parents surely wouldn't charge you for the basics now would they? But, what if your parents didn't have the money for their own basic living expenses, let alone yours, and sold you into bondage? That's what happens to a Pakistani boy named Iqbal. But Iqbal has such amazing talent for weaving the most intricate carpet patterns that many of the carpet dealers wanted to indenture him. But they soon find out that Iqbal is not a quiet and meek child in bondage. He is stubborn and proud and his behavior in unpredictable. A young girl who is also in bondage to the same carpet factory owner tells Iqbal's story. She tells how Iqbal's quiet resistance fuels the children's desire to be free, but they are not as brave as Iqbal. Iqbal's quiet resistance infuriates the owner and results in harsher treatment for all of the indentured children. The day Iqbal slashes in half the elaborately designed rug that the owner already had a buyer for resulted in all of them being punished. Hungry and scared, will the other children continue to support Iqbal's resistance, or will they band against him because he is making their life more difficult?

Excerpt: Pages 9 through 13.

Curriculum Connection: Social Studies
Have students use library media center resources to research child workers in Pakistan and Iqbal's fate after he escaped from bondage. Have them discuss the role Iqbal played in changing the treatment of children in bondage. Have the working conditions improved for these children?

Similar Titles:
Fisher, Susan Staples, ***Shabanu: Daughter of the Wind.*** Laurel Leaf, 2003, 288pp. $6.50. ISBN: 0440238560. Recorded Books, 1995. $44.00. ISBN: 0788701894.
Harlow, Joan Hiatt, ***Joshua's Song.*** Simon & Schuster, 2001, 192pp. $16.00. ISBN: 0689841191. Aladdin, 2003, 160pp. $4.99. ISBN: 0689855427.
Kielburger, Craig, ***Free the Children: A Young Man Fights Against Child Labor and Proves That Children Can Change the World.*** HarperCollins, 1999, 336pp. $13.00. ISBN: 0060930659.
Kuklin, Susan, ***Iqbal Masih and the Crusaders Against Child Slavery.*** Holt, 1998, 144pp. $17.95. ISBN: 0805054596.
Parker, David L., ***Stolen Dreams: Portraits of Working Children.*** Lerner, 1997, 112pp. $14.95. ISBN: 0822529602.

19 Danticat, Edwidge, *Behind the Mountains: The Diary of Celiane Esperance.*

First Person Fiction Series. Orchard, 2002, 224pp. $16.95. ISBN: 0439372992. Scholastic, 2004, 166pp. $6.99. ISBN: 043937300X.

Subjects: Haitians, Immigrants, Moving, Teachers, Violence, Writing
Genres: International, Multicultural, Realistic
Levels: K 5-9, PW 6-10, SLJ 5 up, V 6-9

Annotation: Celiane chronicles her life in Haiti. When Celiane and her mother are victims of a politically motivated bomb blast that puts them in the hospital, the family decides it is time they move to Brooklyn to be with her father.

Booktalk: When I woke up in the hospital I didn't know what day it was or where I was. The last thing I remember was a loud bang and people screaming. The nurse kept telling me to rest, but no one would answer me when I asked about Manman. Finally a nurse came in and asked me my name and where I lived and I told her about Tante Rose. She said that maybe my head wouldn't work right because of the explosion. What explosion? I thought there was a collision – that a big truck hit us from behind. But she told me it was a pipe bomb – something to do with the Haitian election. What did Manman and I have to do with the election? We were just going home from Tante Rose's house. And where is Manman? No one will tell me. Does she have a bandage on her head and a sore neck and not know where I am either?

Excerpt: From break on page 3 to break on page 6.

Curriculum Connection: Social Studies
Edwidge Danticat was born in Haiti and immigrated to the United States when she was a child. Have the students use library media center resources to research the current political conditions in Haiti and how they impact families trying to leave the country.

Similar Titles:
Alvarez, Julia, ***Before We Were Free.*** Random House, 2002, 176pp. $15.95. ISBN: 0375815449. Bantam Doubleday Dell, 2004, 192pp. $5.99. ISBN: 044023784X. Random House Audio, 2004. $25.00. ISBN: 1400085284.
Hodge, Merle, ***For the Life of Leatitia.*** Farrar, Straus & Giroux, 1994, 224pp. $6.95. ISBN: 0374424446.
Osa, Nancy, ***Cuba 15.*** Random House, 2003, 256pp. $15.95. ISBN: 0385730217. Random House, 2005, 304pp. $7.95. ISBN: 0385732333.
Viencenia-Saurez, Ana, ***The Flight to Freedom.*** First Person Fiction Series. Orchard, 2002, 208pp. $16.95. ISBN: 0439381991. Scholastic, 2004, 240pp. $6.99. ISBN: 0439382009.
Wolkstein, Diane, ***Magic Orange Tree: And Other Haitian Folktales.*** Random House, 1997, 212pp. $14.00. ISBN: 0805210776.

De Guzman, Michael, *Beekman's Big Deal.*

Farrar, Straus & Giroux, 2004, 213pp. $16.00. ISBN: 0374306729.

Subjects: Bullies, Fathers and Sons, Friendship, Moving, Schools
Genres: Realistic
Levels: BL 5-8, K 5 up, PW 5 up, SLJ 5-8

Annotation: Twelve-year-old Beekman O'Day is tired of his father's deals not going right, forcing them to change residences frequently. Beekman is again enrolled in a different New York City private school where he is chosen as the bully's newest target.

Booktalk: Beekman had enough. He had never questioned his father about the Big Deals he kept talking about. Beekman had never been to his father's office. He didn't even know where it was. All he ever saw was his father get dressed in a suit every morning and walk up the street one way, while Beekman headed off the other way to yet another private school his father had made some kind of deal to get him into. Beekman never stayed long at any one school because his father's Big Deals more often fell through than worked and Beekman was kicked out for lack of tuition payments. Beekman was sick of moving and sick of changing schools. He decided it was time to find out what this dealing was that his father was doing, so he decided to play hooky and follow him. What Beekman found out confirmed his deepest fears – there were no Big Deals. They were all little deals. Who in their right mind wanted singing fur covered toilet seats anyway? Apparently not even a buyer in Alaska. How soon would it be before Beekman got kicked out of Last Chance Academy? Was there anything Beekman could do to stop it? Maybe he could just refuse to move when his dad said it was time.

Excerpt: Page 12, first paragraph to page 15, end of second full paragraph.

Curriculum Connection: Math

Beekman and his father lived in various locations around the greater New York City area. Have students use library media center and Internet resources to research the New York City neighborhoods and their transportation options, select a neighborhood at least 15 city blocks away from the school of choice, and calculate the distance and time it would take to get to school using the various forms of transportation available.

Similar Titles:

Danziger, Paula, ***This Place Has No Atmosphere.*** Putnam, 1999, 156pp. $4.99. ISBN: 069811695X.

De Guzman, Michael, ***Melonhead.*** Farrar, Straus & Giroux, 2002, 224pp. $17.00. ISBN: 0374349444.

Kehret, Peg, ***Stranger Next Door.*** Dutton, 2002, 160pp. $15.99. ISBN: 0525468293. Penguin, 2003, 176pp. $5.99. ISBN: 0142501786.

Konigsburg, E.L., ***From the Mixed-Up Files of Mrs. Basil E. Frankweiler.*** Simon & Schuster, 2002, 176pp. $16.95. ISBN: 068985322X. Simon & Schuster, 2002, 208pp. $5.99. ISBN: 0689853548. Random House Audio, 1995. $18.00. ISBN: 0807275565. Random House Audio, 2004. $14.99. CD. ISBN: 1400085020.

Pinkwater, Daniel M., ***Looking for Bobowicz: A Hoboken Chicken Story.*** HarperCollins, 2004, 208pp. $16.89. ISBN: 0060535555. HarperAudio, 2004. $22.00. CD. ISBN: 006072286X.

Deak, Erzsi and Kristin Embry-Litchman, eds., *Period Pieces: Stories for Girls.*

HarperCollins, 2003, 144pp. $16.89. ISBN: 0066237971.

Web Site: <http://erzsideak.com>
Subjects: Menstruation, Mothers and Daughters, Sexuality
Genres: Multicultural, Realistic, Short Stories
Levels: BL 4-8, K 4-8, SLJ 4-8

Annotation: Twelve female authors, Linda Sue Park, Rita Williams-Garcia, Johanna Hurwitz and others, shares stories based on their personal experience with their first menstrual period.

Booktalk: Why do the most embarrassing moments happen around a guy you don't know? There I was, horseback riding of all things, when it happened. I was feeling kind of sick to my stomach before the rain hit and I really wanted this supposedly beautiful ride through the mountains to be over with very soon, if not now. The slow gallop was making my stomach feel even worse. The fast gallop about did me in. Red faced, I had to ask Ryan to stop. I got up the courage and announced, "I have to go pee." He was a gentleman about it and turned his back on me as I entered the woods, but my face was beet red. That wasn't bad enough – when I got behind the tree to relieve myself I realized the problem was much worse than I thought.

Excerpt: Page 69.

Curriculum Connection: Language Arts
Have students use library media center resources to research the childhood of the author of one of the short stories and write the dialog that might occur if they were a character in the story and the two of them were interacting.

Similar Titles:
Blackstone, Margaret and Elissa Haden Guest, *Girl Stuff: A Survival Guide to Growing Up.* Harcourt, 2000, 144pp. $14.95. ISBN: 0152018301. Harcourt, 2000, 144pp. $8.95. ISBN: 0152026444.
Gravelle, Karen, Jennifer Gravelle and Debbie Palen, *The Period Book: Everything You Don't Want to Ask (But Need to Know).* Walker, 1996, 128pp. $15.95. ISBN: 0802784208. Walker, 1996, 117pp. $8.95. ISBN: 0802774784.
Holyoke, Nancy, *Yikes!: A Smart Girl's Guide to Surviving Tricky, Sticky, Icky Situations.* Pleasant Company Publications, 2002, 88pp. $8.95. ISBN: 1584855304.
Jukes, Mavis, *It's a Girl Thing: Straight Talk About First Bras, First Periods, and Your Changing Body.* Knopf, 1998, 72pp. $10.00. ISBN: 0679890270.
Mosatche, Harriet S. and Karen Unger, *Too Old For This, Too Young For That!: Your Survival Guide For the Middle-School Years.* Free Spirit, 1999, 200pp. $14.95. ISBN: 1575420678.

22

Dodd, Quentin, *The Princess of Neptune.*
Farrar, Straus & Giroux, 2004, 212pp. $17.00. ISBN: 0374361193.

Web Site: <www.quentindodd.com>
Subjects: Brothers and Sisters, Extraterrestrials, Journeys, Music, Schools, Teachers
Genres: Humor, Mystery, Science Fiction
Levels: BL 5-8, K 5-8, PW 5 up, SLJ 4-6

Annotation: Middle schooler Theora and her younger brother Verb are transported to Jupiter so Theora can compete in an intergalactic beauty contest and they end up helping solve the mystery of who kidnapped the reigning queen, Hortense Benway, a giant singing cockroach.

Booktalk: Science fiction books are supposed to make you think about the future and all the cool gadgets that have been designed. Serious stuff – right? Well, seriousness is not quite the mind set in *The Princess of Neptune*. Granted, there are some pretty interesting futurist devices described, but you might not notice them all while you are laughing over the antics of the characters, or I should say creatures, in this book. Imagine you are transported to Neptune, as a contestant in the annual beauty contest, and are befriended by a couple of "hey dude" king-sized cockroach twins who run the local burger joint. Makes you wonder who is in the kitchen at your favorite burger place, doesn't it? There you are, anticipating the beautiful alien creatures you will be competing against when out comes Hortense Benway, the reigning queen. Don't laugh now, but she is one giant-size singing cockroach and the twins think she is the hottest thing in the galaxy. How does a mere human compete against such beauty?

Excerpt: Page 64 through page 68, third paragraph.

Curriculum Connection: Science
Theora does her science report on Big Phil, Lake Philodendron's version of the Loch Ness Monster. Have students use library media center resources to select and research an unexplained phenomenon, highlighting the scientific evidence that refutes or supports the current beliefs of its existence.

Similar Titles:
Clements, Andrew, ***Things Not Seen.*** Philomel, 2002, 251pp. $15.99. ISBN: 0399236260. Penguin Putnam, 2004, 176pp. $5.99. ISBN: 0142400769. Random House Audio, 2004. $38.00. ISBN: 1400090148.
Dodd, Quentin, ***Beatnik Rutabagas From Beyond the Stars.*** Farrar, Straus & Giroux, 2001, 224pp. $17.00. ISBN: 0374305153.
Korman, Gordon, ***No More Dead Dogs.*** Hyperion, 2000, 180pp. $15.99. ISBN: 0786805315. Hyperion 2002, 192pp. $5.99. ISBN: 0786816015. Recorded Books, 2001. $28.00. ISBN: 0788751042.

Pinkwater, Daniel M., ***5 Novels: Alan Mendelsohn, The Boy From Mars, Slaves of Spiegel, The Last Guru, The Snarkout Boys and The Avocado of Death.*** Farrar, Straus & Giroux, 1997, 648pp. $11.95. ISBN: 0374423296.

Pratchett, Terry, ***The Bromeliad Trilogy: Truckers, Diggers, and Wings.*** HarperCollins, 2003, 512pp. $17.99. ISBN: 0060094931.

Dorros, Arthur, *Under the Sun.*

Abrams, 2004, 224pp. $16.95. ISBN: 0810949334.

Web Site: <www.arthurdorros.com>
Subjects: Death, Journeys, Mothers and Sons, Prejudices, Refugees, Sexual Assault, Survival, Violence, War
Genres: International, Multicultural, Realistic
Levels: BL 6-9, K 5-10, SLJ 6-9

Annotation: Thirteen-year-old Ehmet and his mother leave war-torn Sarajevo to live with relatives, but the soldiers find them and assault his mother. She escapes only to die of pneumonia. Ehmet ends up in a refugee camp but is reunited eventually with his father.

Booktalk: Ehmet and his mother had an agreed upon code and meeting place if something happened. But when Ehmet hears her call out, "Water Man, Water Man!" his first impulse was to run downstairs and see what was happening. He could hear strange voices and glass breaking. Ehmet heard his mother frantically call out again, "Water Man, Water Man!" – their agreed upon code – his nickname because he always carried the water to their apartment in Sarajevo. Ehmet jammed his feet into his running shoes, grabbed his backpack, and climbed through the window and out onto the roof. As he ran across the roof and jumped to the ground he heard the soldiers shouting at him to stop and felt the reverberations of the bullets in the air around him. Ehmet hit the ground running and didn't stop until he was at their secret meeting place. It wasn't until dawn the next day that he saw his mother stumbling toward him. Her clothes were torn and her eyes were glazed over and she had a bruise forming under one of them. Blood had dried under her nose and her face was full of scratches. Before Ehmet could reach out to hold her, his mother walked waist deep into the freezing cold river. She stood in the icy water for what seemed like hours to Ehmet before she finally waded back to shore and collapsed on the ground. Ehmet knew that his mother would never be the same again.

Excerpt: Third paragraph on page 14 to the last paragraph on page 15.

Curriculum Connection: Social Studies
Have students use library media center resources to compare up-to-date maps of the

area Ehmet lived in with maps from 20 years ago and discuss how political boundary changes have affected the people who live there.

Similar Titles:
Filipovic, Zlata, ***Zlata's Diary: A Child's Life in Sarajevo.*** Penguin, 1995, 197pp. $11.00. ISBN: 0140242058. Recorded Books, 1994. $26.00. ISBN: 0788700839.
Fireside, Harvey, ***Young People from Bosnia Talk about War.*** Enslow, 1996, 104pp. $18.85. ISBN: 0894907301.
Gabrielpillai, Matilda, ***Bosnia and Herzegovina.*** Garth Steven, 2001, 96pp. $39.26. ISBN: 083682329X.
Nicholson, Michael, ***Sarajevo: Natasha's Story.*** Hyperion, 1997, 208pp. $9.95. ISBN: 0786882344.
Tekavec, Valerie, ***Teenage Refugees from Bosnia-Herzegovina Speak Out.*** Rosen, 1997, 64pp. $26.50. ISBN: 0823925609.

24 Durbin, William, *The Darkest Evening.*

Scholastic, 2004, 232pp. $15.95. ISBN: 0439373077.
Web Site: <www.williamdurbin.com>
Subjects: Baseball, Brothers and Sisters, Communism, Moving, Music, Prejudices, Survival, Violence
Genres: Historical, International, Multicultural
Levels: BL 5-7, K 5-9, SLJ 6-9

Annotation: Fourteen-year-old Finnish-American Jake Maki and his family move to Russia in the 1930s. Only Jake, his mother, and his little sister are able to escape Stalin's purging of the emigrants by skiing to freedom across the border into Finland.

Booktalk: I cannot believe Father is really going to do this! He has been talking about moving to Russia ever since those Russians have been coming to Minnesota and promising us Finns a better life – something they call a Finnish state in Russia. I don't want to move to Russia. Sure, things are hard now with the economy the way it is, but I love playing baseball in the summer and skiing in the winter. How am I going to hear the World Series on the radio if he takes us to Russia? And of course, Maija agrees with everything Father wants. She's my spoiled little sister – the little princess who can do no wrong. Then there are us two boys. In this family I am the son who argues, and Peter is the smart son, smart also because he says little. But, Peter will wish he had spoken up about not wanting to move to Russia after the Maki family settles in Russia and Peter learns that the promise of musical training is as false as many of the other promises the Russian recruiters made to the Finnish-American families they convinced to move to Russia. And then the Finns, from both America and Finland, start disappearing. Who's next? Jake fears it will be his outspoken father.

Excerpt: Pages 9 through 12.

Curriculum Connection: Social Studies
Many Finns, disillusioned with the lack of jobs in the U.S. during the Depression, moved to Russia. Have students use library media center resources to research the planned Finnish State in Russia and how Stalin's attempt to "purify" the Communist Party affected the Finns living in Russia.

Similar Titles:
Biesanz, Mavis Hiltunen, ***Helmi Mavis: A Finnish-American Girlhood.*** North Star Press of St. Cloud, 1989, 199pp. $12.95. ISBN: 0878390529.
Durbin, William, ***The Journal of Otto Peltonen: A Finnish Immigrant: Hibbing Minnesota, 1905.*** My Name is America Series. Scholastic, 2000, 208pp. $10.95. ISBN: 043909254X. Scholastic, 2003, 208pp. $12.95. ISBN: 0439555000.
Durbin, William, ***Song of Sampo Lake.*** Random House, 2002, 224pp. $15.95. ISBN: 0385327315. Random House, 2004, 224pp. $5.50. ISBN: 0440228999.
Holm, Jennifer L., ***Our Only May Amelia.*** HarperCollins, 1999, 253pp. $15.89. ISBN: 0060283548. HarperCollins, 2001, 272pp. $5.99. ISBN: 0064408566. Random House Audio, 2000. $22.00. ISBN: 0807282340.
Sevander, Mayme, ***They Took My Father: Finnish Americans in Stalin's Russia.*** University of Minnesota Press, 2004, 208pp. $16.95. ISBN: 0816643369.

Edwards, Julie Andrews and Emma Walton Hamilton, *Dragon: Hound of Honor.*

HarperCollins, 2004, 179pp. $16.99. ISBN: 0060571209. HarperCollins, 2005, 256pp. $6.99. ISBN: 0060571217.

Web Site: <www.julieandrewsedwardsbooks.com>
Subjects: Dogs, Friendship, Grieving, Knights and Knighthood, Middle Ages, Murder
Genre: Historical, International, Mystery
Levels: BL 4-8, PW 5 up, PW 4 up, SLJ 5-8

Annotation: This adaptation of the 14th century French Legend of the Dog of Montargis relates the tale of Dragon, a wolfhound that is the only witness to the murder of the young knight Aubrey de Montdidier. Thirteen-year-old Thierry, ward to the Count of Montargis, narrates the tale.

Booktalk: I was on my way back from the stables when his horse galloped into the courtyard, eyes wild. It took me quite some time to calm the horse down and I couldn't help but wonder what he would say if he could talk. His master has been missing for three days and we all feared the worst. We were told marauders had been spotted on the road to Montargis. What if Montdidier had encountered them? After getting the horse settled into the stables I had barely fallen asleep when I head a soft whining at the door. It was Dragon, Montdidier's wolfhound. He was shivering with fear and covered with mud, leaves, and blood. When I cleaned the blood off of him it was clear that Dragon had been slashed several times, with a very sharp blade. I shuddered as I envisioned how he might have gotten these cuts while defending Montdidier from his attackers. I may have initially wished that Montdidier's horse could talk, but Dragon is the one who knows what happened to the missing knight.

Excerpt: Page 41 to the break on page 45.

Curriculum Connection: Language Arts
Have students select an entry from the Glossary of Medieval Terms and use dictionaries and other resources in the library media center to research the history of the term, comparing it to modern terms used today.

Similar Titles:
Cadnum, Michael, ***Book of the Lion.*** Viking, 2000, 156pp. $15.99. ISBN: 0670883867. Penguin, 2001, 208pp. $5.99. ISBN: 0142300349. Recorded Books, 2003. $37.00. ISBN: 1402555393.
Morris, Gerald, ***Parsifal's Page.*** The Squire's Tales Series. Houghton Mifflin, 2001, 240pp. $16.00. ISBN: 0618055096. Houghton Mifflin, 2004, 240pp. $5.95. ISBN: 061843237X.
Pierce, Tamora, ***Squire.*** The Protector of the Small Series. Random House, 2001, 224pp. $17.99. ISBN: 0679989161. Random House, 2002, 432pp. $5.99. ISBN: 0679889191.
Skurzynski, Gloria, ***Spider's Voice.*** Simon & Schuster, 1999, 208pp. $16.95. ISBN: 0689821492.
Yolen, Jane, ***Queen's Own Fool.*** Philomel, 2000, 390pp. $19.99. ISBN: 0399233806. Putnam, 2001, 400pp. $7.99. ISBN: 0698119185.

26 Farmer, Nancy, *The House of the Scorpion.*

Simon & Schuster, 2002, 400pp. $17.95. ISBN: 0689852223. Simon & Schuster, 2004, 380pp. $7.99. ISBN: 0689852231. Recorded Books, 2004. $29.99. ISBN: 1402541732.

Subjects: Drugs, Fathers and Sons, Medical Experimentation, Self-Identity
Genres: Multicultural, Science Fiction
Awards: 2003 Printz Honor, 2003 Newbery Honor
Lists: 2003 BBYA, 2003 CN, 2004 YAC
Levels: BL 7-10, K 6 up, PW 6 up, SLJ 6-10

Annotation: Matt, a clone of 142-year-old El Patron, the drug lord of Opium, a land between the U.S. and Mexico borders, fights for his identity as a human rather than as a donor of body parts.

Booktalk: Imagine that you found out your father was 142 years old. Before you can even absorb the fact that your father is that old, add that you had no human mother and your father is waiting for you to age to the point where he can harvest your heart. Pretty scary scenario isn't it? Welcome to Matt's world. As a young child he lived a sheltered life with his caretaker Celia, in the land of Opium, and had no idea he was anything other than a regular boy. He didn't think anything about the fact that he had a property stamp on his foot. He thought everybody had one. He assumed that all boys had caretakers who made sure they didn't go outside alone. But his whole world changes when he hears a girl's voice outside the window of their little house. Celia isn't around so Matt decides to break out of his confinement and meet this girl who wants him to come out to play with her. The voice he hears is Maria's – the girl who will change his life and perhaps even help him escape from Opium.

Excerpt: First paragraph page 71 through page 74.

Curriculum Connection: Science
Have students use library media center and Internet resources to research recent experimentation in animal cloning and engage in debate as to whether they think this medical practice is ethical.

Similar Titles:
Card, Orson Scott, ***Ender's Game.*** Tor, 1991, 226pp. $24.95. ISBN: 0312932081. Starscape Books, 2002, 336pp. $5.99. ISBN: 0765342294. Audio Renaissance, 2004. $39.95. CD. ISBN: 1593974744.
Colfer, Eoin, ***The Supernaturalist.*** Hyperion, 2004, 272pp. $16.95. ISBN: 0786851481. Miramax, 2005, 272pp. $7.99. ISBN: 078685149X. Listening Library, 2004. $28.00. ISBN: 1400090326.
Layne, Steven L., ***This Side of Paradise.*** Pelican, 2003, 224pp. $15.99. ISBN: 1589800966.
L'Engle, Madeleine, ***A Swiftly Tilting Planet.*** Farrar, Straus & Giroux, 1978, 278pp. $18.00. ISBN: 0374373620. Random House, 1978, 272pp. $5.99. ISBN: 0440901588. Random House Audio, 2002. $30.00. ISBN: 0807209163.
Philbrick, Rodman, ***The Last Book in the Universe.*** Scholastic, 2000, 223pp. $16.95. ISBN: 0439087589. Random House Audio, 2004. $30.00. ISBN: 0807288438.

27 Farmer, Nancy, *The Sea of Trolls.*

Atheneum, 2004, 459pp. $17.95. ISBN: 0689867441. Recorded Books, 2004. $29.99. CD. ISBN: 1402593449.

Subjects: Brothers and Sisters, Folklore, Gods and Goddesses, Journeys, Kidnapping, Magic, Occupations, Wizards
Genres: Adventure, Fantasy, International
Lists: 2005 BBYA, 2005 CN
Levels: BL 6-9, K 5-8, PW 5-8, SLJ 5-9

Annotation: Eleven-year-old Jack, a wizard apprentice, and his little sister, Lucy, are captured by Vikings in the year 793 A.D. They encounter dragons, trolls, and myriad other mythical creatures before they return to their Saxon homeland, with Jack a full-fledged wizard after saving his sister from the Troll Queen.

Booktalk: Jack was more than a little surprised when the Bard asked him if he wanted to be his apprentice. Jack's father didn't think Jack would amount to much so Jack had begun to believe it as well. But the Bard didn't. The Bard knew something about Jack that Jack didn't – something that made the wizard believe in this young farm boy. So Jack became the Bard's apprentice and began to learn about magic and wizardry. But he certainly didn't have the skill to stop the hoard of Vikings who came marauding up the road. He was hoping the fog would hide him and his little sister Lucy, but that wasn't to be. Not with Lucy shouting to them at the top of her lungs, "Here I am!" Lucy was sure they were knights coming to take her back to her castle. See what happens when you let a little girl with a big mouth believe she is a princess who has been taken away from her castle? Those fairy tales their father had filled Lucy's head with had just cost them their freedom. The last thing Jack remembered before he woke up on the Viking ship was a vicious thwonk on the top of his head. Was Lucy on the ship with him? If so, how was he going to save her from these savages?

Excerpt: Pages 87 through 91.

Curriculum Connections: Math, Social Studies
Have students use library media center resources to locate maps of northern Europe and Scandinavia and discuss the possible sea routes the Vikings may have taken from Britain to their homeland. Choosing ports in each country, have students determine how many nautical miles it is between the ports in England and Sweden and how long it may have taken the Vikings to make these voyages.

Similar Titles:
Branford, Henrietta, ***Fated Sky.*** Candlewick, 1999, 160pp. $16.99. ISBN: 0763607754.
Cadnum, Michael, ***Daughter of the Wind.*** Orchard, 2003, 272pp. $17.95. ISBN: 043935224X.

Margeson, Susan M., *Viking.* Eyewitness Books. Dorling Kindersley, 2000, 64pp. $19.99. ISBN: 07896599X.

Picard, Barbara Leonie, *Tales of the Norse Gods.* Oxford University Press, 2001, 160pp. $10.95. ISBN: 0192751166.

Wilmot-Buxton, E.M., *Viking Gods and Heroes.* Dover, 2004, 160pp. $6.95. ISBN: 0486437043.

Feinstein, John, *Last Shot.*

The Final Four Mystery Series. Knopf, 2005, 256pp. $16.95. ISBN: 0375831681. Random House Audio, 2005. $26.00. ISBN: 140009934X. Random House Audio, 2005. $30.00. CD. ISBN: 0307206440.

Subjects: Basketball, Crime, Friendship, Gambling, Occupations, Writing
Genres: Mystery, Realistic, Sports
Levels: PW 5 up, SLJ 6-10

Annotation: Eighth-graders Stevie and Susan Carol, winners of the U.S. Basketball Writer's Association 14-and-under writing contest, discover a blackmail scheme to throw the Final Four championship basketball game in New Orleans and help stop it.

Booktalk: Future sports writers Stevie and Susan Carol had ALL ACCESS passes into the Final Four Basketball Championship. These passes allowed them into the locker rooms and areas where the sportscasters and commentators congregated. But, it wasn't a famous sportscaster that Stevie wanted to meet; it was his favorite basketball player, Chip Graber from Minnesota State. He wanted to interview him for his newspaper column, which was part of his "prize" as one of the winners of the U.S. Basketball Writer's Association writing contest. Stevie and Susan Carol began to explore the stadium, hoping they would find some of the players, and found themselves near the back entrance where the CBS vans were unloading their equipment. They didn't know if they were really allowed in this area or not so they slipped in quietly and were standing where no one could see them when they heard voices. Hiding further behind the equipment, they heard Chip Graber's voice, but before Stevie could even think to step out and intercept him for an interview, they heard someone threatening the basketball star. This guy was actually telling the lead player for the Minnesota State basketball team that he had to throw the final game to Duke – if he didn't the consequences would not only impact Chip, they would ruin his father's coaching career.

Excerpt: Ninth paragraph on page 52 to page 57.

Curriculum Connections: Career Education, Language Arts, Physical Education
Stevie and Susan Carol are interested in careers as sports writers. Have students use library media resources to research other sports-related careers that involve writing.

Similar Titles:
Brooks, Bruce, ***The Moves Make the Man.*** HarperCollins, 1984, 208pp. $16.89. ISBN: 0060206985. HarperCollins, 1996, 288pp. $5.99. ISBN: 0064405648. Recorded Books, 1997. $51.00. ISBN: 0788708295.
Craig, Steve, ***Sportswriting: A Beginner's Guide.*** Discover Writing Press, 2001, 120pp. $15.00. ISBN: 0965657493.
Deuker, Carl, ***Night Hoops.*** Houghton Mifflin, 2000, 256pp. $15.00. ISBN: 0395979366. HarperCollins, 2001, 256pp. $5.99. ISBN: 0064472752.
Herzog, Brad, ***Hoopmania: The Book of Basketball History and Trivia.*** Sports Illustrated for Kids Books. Rosen, 2002, 176pp. $32.60. ISBN: 082393697X.
Soto, Gary, ***Taking Sides.*** Harcourt, 1991, 144pp. $17.00. ISBN: 0152840761. Harcourt, 2003, 144pp. $5.95. ISBN: 0152046941. Recorded Books, 1999. $29.00. ISBN: 0788735160.

29 Fisher, Catherine, ***The Oracle Betrayed.***

The Oracle Prophecies Series. Greenwillow, 2004, 341pp. $17.89. ISBN: 0060571586. HarperCollins, 2005, 352pp. $5.99. ISBN: 0060571594.

Subjects: Gods and Goddesses, Murder, Religion, Self-Esteem
Genres: Fantasy, Mystery
Lists: 2005 BBYA, 2005 CN
Levels: BL 5-8, K 5 up, PW 5 up, SLJ 5-9, V 6-12

Annotation: In Two Lands, a world similar to ancient Greece, Mirany is the Bearer of the ceremonial bowl that holds the God-on-Earth in his deadly scorpion form. Mirany becomes embroiled in an attempt to stop a treasonous military leader and the unscrupulous Speaker from appointing their own Archon, the human embodiment of the god.

Booktalk: Mirany wondered why she was chosen to be the new attendant to the Speaker. She was a novice from a distant land and the other girls resented Mirany for getting the prestigious position. So why did the now dead Archon, once the human vessel for the god, thrust a note into her hand and warn her of the treachery around her? And why was the god speaking to Mirany through her own mind? Until she heard his voice inside her head she wasn't even sure he existed, but now she had no choice but to believe in him. She knew she wasn't going crazy – the voice she heard was the Archon's and he needed her help. It would not be long for Mirany to discover that the Speaker, who should be the one hearing the Archon in her head was not. She was just pretending to hear him, but what the Speaker said she heard and what the Archon was telling Mirany were nothing alike. Mirany knew treason was in the air. She was hearing the Archon's request loud and clear and didn't like what he was telling her she must do.

Excerpt: Page 12, third full paragraph, to the break on page 14.

Curriculum Connections: Science, Social Studies
The setting for this book is reminiscent of Greece but the burial rites are more like those of the ancient Egyptians. Have students use library media center resources to research the burial rites of both the ancient Greeks and the ancient Egyptians. Lead a class discussion to compare the culturally specific rituals and procedures used, creating a comparison chart.

Similar Titles:
Cooney, Caroline B., ***For All Time.*** Bantam Doubleday Dell, 2001, 272pp. $17.99. ISBN: 0385900198. Bantam Doubleday Dell, 2003, 272pp. $4.99. ISBN: 0440229316.
Cooney, Caroline B., ***Goddess of Yesterday.*** Bantam Doubleday Dell, 2002, 272pp. $15.95. ISBN: 0385729456. Bantam Doubleday Dell, 2003, 272pp. $5.99. ISBN: 0440229308. Recorded Books, 2003. $54.00. ISBN: 1402546696.
Curry, Jane Louise, ***The Egyptian Box.*** Simon & Schuster, 2002, 192pp. $16.95. ISBN: 0689842732.
Ewing, Lynne, ***The Talisman.*** Daughters of the Moon Series. Hyperion, 2003, 288pp. $9.99. ISBN: 0786818786.
McLaren, Clemence, ***Waiting for Odysseus.*** Simon & Schuster, 2004, 178pp. $5.99. ISBN: 0689867050.

30

Frank, E.R., *Friction.*

Atheneum, 2003, 208pp. $16.95. ISBN: 068985384X. Simon & Schuster, 2004, 208pp. $6.99. ISBN: 0689853858. Random House Audio, 2003. $25.00. ISBN: 080721647X.

Subjects: Child Sexual Abuse, Emotional Problems, Friendship, Schools, Sexuality, Teachers
Genres: Realistic
Lists: 2004 BBYA
Levels: K 6-9, PW 7-up, SLJ 6-10

Annotation: Alex is happy in her 8th grade alternative school until a new student, who is being sexually abused by her father, starts rumors about their young male teacher being attracted to Alex. The accusations result in the teacher leaving his job.

Booktalk: Hi. I'm Alex. Have you ever felt like your life was out of control and there was nothing you could do to stop it? That what you were doing was hurting other people and no matter what you did to try and make it better, it just got worse? The school year started out great. We have this really neat teacher, Simon, who does all kinds of science experiments with us and even takes us on camping trips. By the way, I don't go to a regular school, I go to an alternative school and I am in the 8th grade. We get to call our teachers by their first names. Anyway, everything was going just fine and then Stacy came along. At first I liked hanging around with her. But then she started saying things about me and Simon. Like she said that Simon was in love with me. That's stupid. I'm just a girl and he's a man and besides, he's got a girlfriend. But Stacy wouldn't give up on it – she kept putting these doubts in my head, and then she started telling the other kids too. It's not true, but I think I let it go too far and now Simon might be in trouble. And, I'm partially to blame because I listened to Stacy's lies.

Excerpt: Chapter 3.

Curriculum Connection: Health
Have students use library media center resources to research the changes that happen emotionally and physically when a girl or boy goes through puberty. Have the students discuss how some of the physical changes are obvious, but that the emotional ones may not be so easy to pinpoint. How do these unseen changes affect how they interact with their family and friends?

Similar Titles:
Blume, Judy, ***Are You There God? It's Me, Margaret.*** Simon & Schuster, 2001, 160pp. $17.00. ISBN: 0689415282. Random House, 1986, 160pp. $5.99. ISBN: 0440904193. Random House Audio, 1997. $18.00. ISBN: 0807278599.
Cisneros, Sandra, ***The House on Mango Street.*** Random House, 1994, 134pp. $24.00. ISBN: 067943335X. Knopf, 1991, 128pp. $9.95. ISBN: 0679734775.
Lee, Harper, ***To Kill a Mockingbird.*** HarperCollins, 1999, 323pp. $18.00. ISBN: 0060194995. HarperCollins, 2002, 336pp. $11.95. ISBN: 0060935464.
Naylor, Phyllis Reynolds, ***Simply Alice.*** Simon & Schuster, 2002, 240pp. $16.00. ISBN: 0689826354. Simon & Schuster, 2003, 240pp. $4.99. ISBN: 0689859651.
Speare, Elizabeth George, ***The Witch of Blackbird Pond.*** Houghton Mifflin, 1958, 256pp. $16.00. ISBN: 0395071143. Bantam Doubleday Dell, 1978, 224pp. $6.50. ISBN: 0440995779. Random House Audio, 2002. $26.00. ISBN: 0807207489. Random House Audio, 2004. $45.00. CD. ISBN: 0807216100.

Funke, Cornelia, *The Thief Lord.*

Scholastic, 2002, 352pp. $16.95. ISBN: 0439404371. Scholastic, 2003, 349pp. $6.99. ISBN: 043942089X. Random House Audio, 2002. $30.00. ISBN: 0807209767.

Subjects: Brothers, Crime, Friendship, Grieving, Magic, Orphans, Runaways
Genres: International, Mystery
Lists: 2003 CN
Levels: BL 6-9, K 5-9, LMC 6-12, SLJ 6-8

Annotation: Twelve-year-old Prosper and his five-year-old brother Bo run away to Venice when their aunt tries to separate them after their mother's death. They are taken in by a group of orphans lead by the Thief Lord who they think is a master thief, but is actually the son of rich man who owns the rundown theater they live in. The detective who is hired to find them befriends the brothers.

Booktalk: Do you have younger brothers or sisters? Well, I do. I have a little brother named Bo, who tags along with me everywhere I go. I told my mom I would always take care of Bo, and I have, even after she died. You can't tell anyone, but we ran away to Venice. Mom told us how beautiful it was and she was right. We love it here. We even have our own family now. Sure we may be all orphans who live in a rundown old movie theater but we have the Thief Lord to look after us. He isn't much older than I am but he is a master thief and he makes sure we have enough to eat and even brought us mattresses to sleep on. But, I sure would like to know where he goes at night. He never sleeps in the theater with us and he doesn't talk about his life at all. But that's okay, because most of us don't. We would rather forget why we are orphans living in a deserted theater.

Excerpt: (pbk). Page 8, first full paragraph to break on page 12.

Curriculum Connection: Social Studies
Have students use library media center and Internet resources to research the layout of Venice and how people navigate this city on water. Have them determine how the city has changed over the years and how pollution and flooding of the canals are controlled.

Similar Titles:

Bjork, Christina, ***Vendela in Venice.*** R & S Books, 1999, 96pp. $18.00. ISBN: 912964559X.
Funke, Cornelia, ***Inkheart.*** Scholastic, 2003, 544pp. $19.95. ISBN: 0439531640. Random House Audio, 2003, $39.95. ISBN: 0807219509. Random House Audio, 2003. $75.00. CD. ISBN: 0807220108.
Howe, Norma, ***Blue Avenger Cracks the Code.*** Holt, 2000, 296pp. $17.00. ISBN: 0805063722. Random House Audio, 2000. $32.00. ISBN: 0807287121.
Napoli, Donna Jo, ***Daughter of Venice.*** Random House, 2002, 288pp. $16.95. ISBN: 0385327803. Bantam Doubleday Dell, 2003, 288pp. $5.50. ISBN: 0440229286.
Napoli, Donna Jo, ***For the Love of Venice.*** Random House, 2000, 256pp. $4.99. ISBN: 0440414113.

32 Gaiman, Neil, *Coraline.*

HarperCollins, 2002, 162pp. $15.99. ISBN: 0380977788. HarperCollins, 2003, 162pp. $5.99. ISBN: 0380807343. HarperCollinsAudio, 2002. $18.00. ISBN: 0060504544. HarperCollinsAudio, 2002. $22.00. CD. ISBN: 06051048X.

Web Site: <www.neilgaiman.com>
Subjects: Mothers and Daughters, Self-Identity
Genres: Fantasy, Horror
Lists: 2003 BBYA, 2003 CC, 2003 CN
Levels: BL 5-8, K 4-7, PW 3 up, SLJ 6-8

Annotation: Coraline, a bored and inquisitive girl, enters a door to a mirror universe inhabited by creepy parents with black shiny button eyes who want to keep her there.

Booktalk: Have you ever been so bored that you began to count things? Then even count things of a certain color? That's how bored Coraline was. She had already visited the eccentric neighbors in the other apartments in the old house she and her parents live in. And her parents, as usual, were too busy to spend any time with her. So after counting all the blue doors, 14 to be exact, she decided that she *would* figure out how to get through the final blue door in her house – the very door that normally opened up onto a brick wall. But not this time. This time there was a doorway to an alternate world. At first this new world was lots of fun. Her alternate parents gave her all the attention she wanted. Then Coraline realized that they gave her way too much attention. They were smothering her with attention. She never thought she'd be saying that! Now Coraline wants out of this creepy warped version of her own world, but she doesn't think her new parents with their shiny black button eyes and clinging arms are going to let her leave.

Excerpt: Last full paragraph on page 4 through page 12.

Curriculum Connection: Language Arts

Have students use the library media center online catalog and other resources to locate other books that include alternate worlds or time travel settings. After reading one of the titles they found, have students write stories of what might have happened if the main character in this book found him or herself in an alternate world as did Coraline.

Similar Titles:

Byng, Georgia, ***Molly Moon's Incredible Book of Hypnotism.*** The Molly Moon Series. HarperCollins, 2003, 368pp. $17.89. ISBN: 0060514073. HarperCollins, 2004, 400pp. $6.99. ISBN: 0060514094. HarperCollinsAudio, 2003. $34.95. ISBN: 006054273X.

Dahl, Roald, ***The BFG.*** Farrar, Straus & Giroux, 1982, 221pp. $17.00. ISBN: 0374304696. Puffin, 1998, 208pp. $6.99. ISBN: 0141301058. HarperCollinsAudio, 2002. $22.00. ISBN: 0060091150.

Funke, Cornelia, ***The Dragon Rider.*** Scholastic, 2004, 528pp. $12.95. ISBN: 0439456959. Random House Audio, 2004. $33.00. ISBN: 1400090903.
Gaiman, Neil, ***The Wolves in the Walls.*** HarperCollins, 2003, 56pp. $16.99. ISBN: 038097827X. HarperTrophy, 2005, 56pp. $6.99. ISBN: 0380810956.
Snicket, Lemony, ***The Bad Beginning.*** A Series of Unfortunate Events Series. HarperCollins, 1999, 176pp. $15.89. ISBN: 0060283122. Random House Audio, 2001. $14.99. ISBN: 0807261785. Random House Audio, 2003. $23.95. CD. ISBN: 0807219908.

Gantos, Jack, *Joey Pigza Loses Control.*

Farrar, Straus & Giroux, 2000, 196pp. $16.00. ISBN: 0374399891. HarperTrophy, 2002, 208pp. $5.99. ISBN: 0064410226. Random House Audio, 2000. $22.00. ISBN: 0807261610. Random House Audio, 2004. $30.00. ISBN: 1400086167.

Web Site: <www.jackgantos.com>
Subjects: Alcoholism, Attention Deficit Hyperactivity Disorder, Baseball, Fathers and Sons
Genre: Humor, Realistic, Sports
Awards: 2001 Newbery Honor
Lists: CN 2001
Levels: BL 4-7, PW 5 up, SLJ 4-8, V 5-8

Annotation: Joey spends the summer with his father and becomes the hot-shot pitcher on the baseball team that his dad coaches, but Joey isn't able to keep himself under control when his father convinces Joey that he is "normal" and doesn't need his ADHD medication.

Booktalk: Joey is both excited and apprehensive about spending the summer with his father. His mother is not at all thrilled about the idea. She says his dad is just a bigger version of Joey – like a top about to spin out of control. Joey's dad says that he has his drinking under control, but his mom isn't so sure about that. And Joey isn't sure he wants to be around his grandmother all summer. The last time he was with her she shut him in the refrigerator. But, now that he is the star pitcher on the baseball team his dad coaches, Joey thinks spending the summer with them is great. At first it's no big deal that his dad drinks a bit too much and acts weird at times. Joey is getting to spend time with him and that is what he wanted. But, being around his dad stops being fun when he decides Joey is a "normal" kid. He tells Joey that he just needs to learn to be a man about his problems. Then he throws Joey's ADHD medication down the toilet. Joey knows what's coming. Joey has been through this before and he knows the Tasmanian devil inside of him called ADHD is going to hit like a freight train. Joey feels like a blinded deer on the tracks with nowhere to run.

Excerpt: Page 3 through first paragraph on page 8.

Curriculum Connections: Health, Science

Have students use library media center resources to research other disorders that have similar affects as ADHD, such as obsessive-compulsive disorder. Have students discuss why Joey's dad's idea of "being a man about it" isn't an effective way to deal with ADHD.

Similar Titles:

Gantos, Jack, ***Heads or Tails: Stories from the Sixth Grade.*** Farrar, Straus & Giroux, 1994, 160pp. $16.00. ISBN: 0374329095. Farrar, Straus & Giroux, 1995, 151pp. $5.95. ISBN: 0374429235. Recorded Books, 1997. $35.00. ISBN: 0788711059.

Gantos, Jack, ***Joey Pigza Swallowed the Key.*** Farrar, Straus & Giroux, 1998, 154pp. $16.00. ISBN: 0374336644. HarperTrophy, 2000, 160pp. $5.99. ISBN: 0064408337. Random House Audio, 1999. $18.00. ISBN: 0807281719. Random House Audio, 2004. $30.00. CD. ISBN: 0807220035.

Gantos, Jack, ***What Would Joey Do?*** Farrar, Straus & Giroux, 2002, 240pp. $16.00. ISBN: 0374399867. HarperTrophy, 2004, 240pp. $5.99. ISBN: 0060544031. Random House Audio, 2002. $25.00. ISBN: 0807209481.

Morrison, Jaydene, ***Coping with ADD/ADHD (Attention Deficit Disorder/Attention Deficit Hyperactivity Disorder).*** Rosen, 2000, 128pp. $26.50. ISBN: 082393196X.

Quinn, Patricia O. and Judith M. Stern, ***Putting On the Brakes: Young People's Guide to Understanding Attention Deficit Hyperactivity Disorder.*** American Psychological Association, 1993, 88pp. $14.95. ISBN: 1557988323.

34 Giff, Patricia Reilly, *Pictures of Hollis Woods.*

Random House, 2002, 166pp. $15.95. ISBN: 0385326556. Random House, 2004, 176pp. $6.50. ISBN: 0440415780. Random House Audio, 2002. $25.00. ISBN: 0807209198. Random House Audio, 2004. $24.00. CD. ISBN: 0807217867.

Web Site: <www.patriciareillygiff.com>
Subjects: Artists, Elderly, Foster Homes, Orphans, Runaways, Self-Esteem
Genre: Realistic
Awards: 2003 Newbery Honor
Lists: 2003 BBYA, 2003 CN, 2003 TC
Levels: BL 5-7, K 4-9, PW 4-8, SLJ 4-7

Annotation: Twelve-year-old Hollis Woods runs away from foster homes until she is placed with Josie, a retired art teacher who is becoming so forgetful that Hollis fears Social Services will figure out what is happening and will place her elsewhere so Hollis runs away and takes Josie with her.

Booktalk: Hollis seems to have overcome her need to run away from every foster home she has ever lived in. She has spent the summer exploring the woods with Steven, the son of the family she is living with. She is actually happy while she draws pictures of her new family and the mountain. No worries at this foster home. But, oh, that mountain. It is as if it is pulling at her – something up there is beckoning to her. Even though the Old Man has told both Hollis and Steven that they are not to go to the top of the mountain, Hollis can't let it go. When she asked him why they can't go up there Mr. Regan said that driving up the mountain is much too dangerous. The road is slippery and muddy. But, Hollis really wants to see the top of that mountain. She can't get it out of her head – the need to look down on the property, the summer home of the family who is going to adopt her. So Hollis forces the issue, but what happens on the mountain makes her run away from the Regan family too.

Excerpt: Chapter 1.

Curriculum Connection: Art

After sharing library media center materials with examples of landscape art, have students use the examples to help them create their own landscape painting of the mountain near the Regan home, based on the narrative description in the book.

Similar Titles:

Baillett, Blue, ***Chasing Vermeer.*** Scholastic, 2004, 272pp. $16.95. ISBN: 0439372941. Scholastic, 2005, 272pp. $6.99. ISBN: 0439372976. Random House Audio, 2004. $25.00. ISBN: 0307206726. Random House Audio, 2004. $28.00. CD. ISBN: 0307206734.

Creech, Sharon, ***Ruby Holler.*** HarperCollins, 2002, 320pp. $16.89. ISBN: 0060277335. HarperTrophy, 2004, 320pp. $5.99. ISBN: 0060560150. HarperChildrensAudio, 2002. $25.00. ISBN: 0060087862.

Meyer, Stephanie H., ed., ***Teen Ink: A Collection of Short Stories, Art and Photography.*** Teen Ink Series. Health Communications, 2004, 360pp. $12.95. ISBN 0757300502.

Park, Barbara, ***The Graduation of Jake Moon.*** Simon & Schuster, 2000, 128pp. $15.00. ISBN: 068983912X. Simon & Schuster, 2002, 115pp. $4.99. ISBN: 0689839855. Listening Library, 2000. $18.00. ISBN: 0807261602.

Paterson, Katherine, ***The Great Gilly Hopkins.*** HarperCollins, 1978, 160pp. $16.89. ISBN: 0690038380. HarperTrophy, 1987, 160pp. $5.99. ISBN: 0064402010. Recorded Books, 1997. $35.00. ISBN: 078870740X. Recorded Books, 2000. $39.00. CD. ISBN: 0788747371.

35 Greene, Bette, *I've Already Forgotten Your Name, Philip Hall!*

HarperCollins, 2004, 167pp. $15.99. ISBN: 006058359.

Subjects: African Americans, Friendship, Grandmothers, Relationships, Self-Esteem
Genre: Humor, Multicultural, Realistic
Levels: BL 4-7, PW 5 up, SLJ 4-7, V 6-8

Annotation: Beth Lambert returns to Pocahantas, Arkansas after spending time with her grandmother in a neighboring town only to discover that she still likes Philip Hall, but lets him believe she has a boyfriend who he challenges to an arm wrestling match. Philip's opponent ends up being Beth's grandmother.

Booktalk: You'd think that boy would know he is supposed to follow me when I walk home from church. Where is he anyway? It isn't like I am walking too fast – the only thing faster than Philip Hall is the sheriff's siren-squawking squad car. That Philip Hall had better not be walking her home. I can't even say her name, but let's just say she is in that Pretty Penny group that I used to be the president of – that group that doesn't want me, the founder of the group, as president anymore. Never mind what happened so that the other members voted me out. Right now all I can think about is that Philip Hall. I can't believe he didn't show up! I don't care if I ever hear that no good polecat's voice again! That's when I hear his voice, from up in the tree next to the road! He has heard everything I just said about him and there he sits with a big grin on his face. So now how to I get myself out of this one?

Excerpt: Page 33 to the first paragraph on page 36.

Curriculum Connection: Physical Education
Arm wrestling is a sport that requires only two people. Have students use library media center resources to discover other types of two-person sporting competitions and events and create a handbook of these activities, with directions for each.

Similar Titles:

Bradby, Maria, ***Some Friend.*** Simon & Schuster, 2004, 240pp. $15.95. ISBN: 0689856156.
Creech, Sharon, ***Absolutely Normal Chaos.*** HarperCollins, 1995, 240pp. $16.89. ISBN: 0060269928. HarperCollins, 1997, 230pp. $5.99. ISBN: 0064406326.
Greene, Bette, ***Get On Out of Here, Philip Hall!*** Puffin, 1999, 150pp. $4.99. ISBN: 0141303115.
Greene, Bette, ***Philip Hall Likes Me, I Reckon Maybe.*** Puffin, 1999, 144pp. $5.99. ISBN: 0141303123. Recorded Books, 2001. $32.00. ISBN: 0788745611.
Woodson, Jacqueline, ***Last Summer with Maizon.*** Putnam, 2001, 112pp. $16.99. ISBN: 0399237550. Putnam, 2002, 128pp $4.99. ISBN: 0698119290.

Griffin, Peni R., *11,000 Years Lost.*
Abrams, 2005, 332pp. $18.95. ISBN: 081948222.

Subjects: Ecology, Elderly, Friendship, Journeys, Magic, Prehistoric Man, Sisters, Survival, Time Travel
Genres: Adventure, Fantasy, Historical, Supernatural
Levels: BL 5-8, K 5-9, SLJ 5-7

Annotation: Eleven-year-old Esther Aragones sneaks off to a Texas Hill Country archeological dig site and walks through a time warp door and into the Pleistocene era. She is "adopted" by a Clovis family and learns how to survive where megafauna, such as scimitar cats and giant bears, are a constant threat, as is starvation and the superstitious fears that Esther has come from the stars.

Booktalk: Have you ever been so into something you would rather be involved in it than eat or sleep? Has it ever been something your mother doesn't approve of? Well, that's what happens to Esther and her fascination with the archeological dig site near her home in Texas. After all, Esther is the one who found the first artifact and turned it in to her teacher. She is the one who brought the archeologist to the tiny hidden cave where she found the Clovis point. It's summer vacation and Esther is at the dig site every day. She comes home every evening covered with dust and dirt. Her mother has had enough of it and tells Esther that she is spending the day with her family. But Esther sneaks off to the dig site anyway. On the way she sees two girls, one of them about her age, and a little one, with no clothes on, playing in the meadow. That's strange – no one lets their little sister run around naked. And what is the deal with the sticks they are carrying? Not understanding just how wrong this scene is in modern day Texas, Esther walks out of the woods and into the meadow to talk to the girls. What she doesn't realize, until it is too late, is that she has just walked through a door in time and is now 11,000 years lost in the past.

Excerpt: Seventh paragraph on page 11 to the first paragraph on page 16.

Curriculum Connection: Social Studies
Have students use library media center resources to research the various types of tools prehistoric man created. Have students try to match the prehistoric tools with modern equivalents and discuss which of the tools is more efficient for the intended use.

Similar Titles:
Dickinson, Peter, *A Bone From a Dry Sea.* Bantam Doubleday Dell, 1995, 199pp. $5.50. ISBN: 0440219280.
Dickinson, Peter, *The Kin: Suth's Story.* Putnam, 2003, 640pp. $24.95. ISBN: 0399240225. Puffin, 2003, 640pp. $7.99. ISBN: 0142501204.
Gray, Luli, *Timespinners.* Houghton Mifflin, 2003, 160pp. $15.00. ISBN: 061816412X.

Hapka, Cathy, ***Oasis.*** The Dinotopia Series. Random House, 2002, 208pp. $3.99. ISBN: 037582295X.

Jones, Diana Wynne, ***Cart and Cwidder.*** The Dalemark Quartet Series. HarperCollins, 1995, 224pp. $15.00. ISBN: 0688133606. HarperCollins, 2001, 240pp. $6.95. ISBN: 0064473139.

37 Grossman, David, *Duel.*

Bloomsbury, 2004, 112pp. $15.95. ISBN: 1582349304.

Subjects: Artists, Crime, Elderly, Friendship, Jews, Photography
Genres: Historical, Humor, International, Mystery
Levels: BL 4-7, K 6-8, SLJ 5-7

Annotation: In 1966 Jerusalem, 12-year-old David becomes friends with elderly Mr. Rosenthal, who is challenged to a duel by Mr. Schwartz over the theft of a painting left to him by the woman they both loved. David helps stop the duel and discovers the real thief is the daughter of the artist.

Booktalk: You wouldn't think you could find out too much from underneath a bed, now would you? Although the view is limited, I was very glad to be under Mr. Rosenthal's bed when Mr. Schwartz came to visit. I spend a lot of time in the Jerusalem home for the aged with Mr. Rosenthal. My mom can't figure out why I spend so much time there, but Mr. Rosenthal really is a fun old guy and he has the neatest cameras. But I wasn't sure how I was going to help Mr. Rosenthal when I saw that this other old guy had size 17 shoes! From my point of view, under the bed, they looked awfully big next to Mr. Rosenthal's small worn sneakers that were just inches in front of my face. As I lay there I couldn't see anything but shoes, but I was sure that Schwartz was towering over tiny Mr. Rosenthal. I was relieved to be hiding under the bed when I heard Schwartz's voice, mean and hard, accusing Mr. Rosenthal of stealing his beloved painting of the laughing mouth of a woman both men had loved when they were young. But when Schwartz challenged Mr. Rosenthal to a duel, that's when my breath stopped. A duel? Two old guys in their seventies with guns? This is crazy! But Mr. Rosenthal accepted before I could even think about crawling out from under the bed to protest. It's a matter of honor he said. How am I supposed to stop this? I don't want an old guy's death on my conscience, even if Mr. Rosenthal thinks it is an honorable way to go!

Excerpt: Pages 9 through 13.

Curriculum Connection: Social Studies
Have students use library media center resources to compare the Jerusalem of today with that of David's time, the 1960s. Have them determine if the political climate has changed and whether or not they think life is better or worse for young teens now.

Similar Titles:
Carmi, Daniella, **Samir and Yonatan.** Scholastic, 2000, 183pp. $15.95. ISBN: 0439135044. Scholastic, 2002, 160pp. $4.99. ISBN: 0439135230.
Emmer, E.R., **The Dolphin Project.** Four Corners Publishing, 2005, 202pp. $6.95. ISBN: 1893577120.
Nye, Naomi Shihab, **19 Varieties of Gazelle: Poems of the Middle East.** HarperCollins, 2002, 142pp. $16.89. ISBN: 0060097663. HarperCollins, 2005, 160pp. $6.99. ISBN: 0060504048.
Nye, Naomi Shihab, **Habibi.** Simon & Schuster, 1997, 272pp. $16.00. ISBN: 0689801491. Simon & Schuster, 1999, 271pp. $5.99. ISBN: 0689825234. Recorded Books, 2000. $36.00. ISBN: 0788735322.
Slavik, Diane, **Daily Life in Ancient and Modern Jerusalem.** Lerner, 2000, 64pp. $18.95. ISBN: 0822532182.

Harlow, Joan Hiatt, *Shadows on the Sea.*

Simon & Schuster, 2003, 244pp. $16.95. ISBN: 0689849265. Simon & Schuster, 2005, 256pp. $4.99. ISBN: 0689849273.

Web Site: <www.joanhiattharlow.com>
Subjects: Birds, Crime, Friendship, Grandmothers, War, World War II
Genres: Historical, Mystery
Levels: BL 7-10, K 4-8, PW 4-7, SLJ 6-8

Annotation: In 1942, 14-year-old Jill is sent to live with her grandmother in a remote Maine village and becomes friends with another newcomer, Wendy, whose aunt turns out to be a spy for the Germans.

Booktalk: Initially Jill was not at all happy about the idea of spending the summer with her Nana in a tiny remote village in rural Maine. Why couldn't she have gone with her mother to Newfoundland? But no – her mother said it was too dangerous with the German subs trying to sink American ships at sea. At least worrying about German submarines lurking in the waters around their ship would add some excitement to her life. Jill wants an adventure and she is about to get one in Nana's sleepy seaside village. Jill begins to notice what she considers suspicious activity while she watches the village from the Widow's Walk atop her grandmother's house. Jill enlists the aid of a local boy, Quarry, to help her find out who sent out the carrier pigeon that her grandmother's cat caught. There has to be something going on. Why else would someone have working carrier pigeons in rural Maine? The intrigue thickens when Jill finds a message attached to the bird's leg, a message written in German. As far as Jill is concerned everyone in the village is a suspect, even her own grandmother. After all, Nana does have friends who speak German. Someone in this village is a German spy and Jill is going to find out who.

Excerpt: Page 37, last line, through fourth paragraph on page 41.

Curriculum Connection: Social Studies
Harlow's novel is based on actual events during World War II when German submarines used Maine's remote bays to deliver messages to spies. Have students use library media center resources to research the incident that occurred in Winter Harbor, Maine.

Similar Titles:
Agell, Charlotte, ***Welcome Home or Someplace Like It.*** Holt, 2003, 240pp. $16.95. ISBN: 0805070834.
Greene, Bette, ***Summer of My German Soldier.*** Penguin, 2003, 256pp. $16.99. ISBN: 0803728697. Penguin, 1999, 208pp. $6.99. ISBN: 014130636X. Recorded Books, 1999. $45.00. ISBN: 078870365X.
Hahn, Mary Downing, ***Stepping On the Cracks.*** Houghton Mifflin, 1991, 216pp. $16.00. ISBN: 0395585074. HarperCollins, 1992, 216pp. $5.99. ISBN: 0380719002.
Lisle, Janet Taylor, ***The Art of Keeping Cool.*** Atheneum, 2000, 216pp. $17.00. ISBN: 0689837879. Simon & Schuster, 2002, 256pp. $4.99. ISBN: 0689837887.
Spinelli, Jerry, ***Milkweed.*** Random House, 2003, 224pp. $17.99. ISBN: 0375913742. Random House Audio, 2003. $25.00. ISBN: 0807218588. Random House Audio, 2004. $40.00. CD. ISBN: 0807220019.

39 Hesse, Karen, *Aleutian Sparrow.*

Simon & Schuster, 2003, 158pp. $16.95. ISBN: 0689861893. Simon & Schuster, 2005, 160pp. $5.95. ISBN: 1416903275. Random House Audio, 2003. $12.99. ISBN: 0807219665. Random House Audio, 2004. $24.00. ISBN: 0807220140.

Subjects: Death, Illness, Internment Camps, Moving, Native Americans, Schools, War, World War II
Genres: Historical, Multicultural
Levels: BL 7-12, K 5-10, PW 5-9, SLJ 6 up

Annotation: In free verse, Hesse tells of Vera and the other Aleuts who are relocated to Wrangell, Alaska when the Japanese invade the Aleutian Islands in 1942. Many of the Aleuts die of illness, but Vera is strong and able to return home.

Booktalk: Did you know that the Japanese landed on U.S. soil during World War II? They did. They landed on the remote Alaskan island chain called the Aleutians. To ensure that the Japanese did not have access to supplies or shelter, the U.S. Navy torched entire towns and relocated the Aleuts to internment camps in Southeast Alaska and the Seattle area. Vera is in the group of Aleuts relocated to Wrangell, Alaska with its rainy climate so different from the Aleutians that many of them died from pneumonia. Others died of sheer loneliness for their beloved islands. Many just gave up because they did not know how to survive in a non-Aleutian environment, weather or people wise. But not Vera. She was a strong one. She knew what she wanted and that was to go back home. Even after her best friend died Vera stayed strong and stayed in school, determined to make it back home. Meet Vera – the *Aleutian Sparrow*.

Excerpt: Page 122.

Curriculum Connection: Social Studies
Have students use library media center materials to research what happened to the Aleuts after WWII and determine how many Aleuts were able to return to the Aleutians and what condition their homes were in when they returned. Discuss the affect the relocation had on future generations of Aleuts.

Similar Titles:
Bowermaster, Jon, ***Aleutian Adventure: Kayaking in the Birthplace of the Winds.*** National Geographic, 2001, 64pp. $17.95. ISBN: 0792279999.
Griese, Arnold A., ***A Wind Is Not a River.*** Boyd Mills, 1996, 128pp. $9.95. ISBN: 1563975645.
Patneaude, David, ***Thin Wood Walls.*** Houghton Mifflin, 2004, 240pp. $16.00. ISBN: 0618342907.
Walters, Eric, ***War of the Eagles.*** Orca, 1998, 160pp. $14.00. ISBN: 1551431181. Orca, 1998, 224pp. $7.95. ISBN: 1551430991.
Wolff, Virginia Euwer, ***Bat 6.*** Scholastic, 1998, 240pp. $16.95. ISBN: 0590897993. Random House Audio, 2004. $30.00. ISBN: 0807282219.

40

Hiaasen, Carl, *Hoot.*

Knopf, 2002, 304pp. $15.95. ISBN: 0375821813. Knopf, 2004, 304pp. $8.95. ISBN: 0375829164. Random House Audio, 2002. $26.00. ISBN: 0807209228. Random House Audio, 2004. $29.95. CD. ISBN: 0307206971.

Web Site: <www.carlhiaasen.com>
Subjects: Birds, Bullies, Ecology, Endangered Species, Friendship, Moving, Runaways
Genres: Humor, Mystery, Realistic
Awards: 2003 Newbery Honor
Lists: 2003 BBYA, 2003 CN, 2003 TC, 2004 YAC
Levels: BL 5-8, K 5-9, PW 5 up, SLJ 6-9

Annotation: Roy Eberhardt is a new kid at the Middle School in Coconut Grove, Florida and the prime target for Dana Matherson, the class bully. Coconut Grove is also the site for a new Mother Paula's All-American Pancake House. Roy discovers a runaway boy living in the swamp who makes nocturnal visits to the restaurant's construction site, armed with snakes and alligators, intent on stopping construction to protect the endangered burrowing owls that live there.

Booktalk: Dana Matherson had been beating Roy up almost every morning on the bus. It was one of those miserable mornings, with his face mashed up against the window, that Roy saw the tall skinny barefoot boy run by. This kid wasn't running toward school, he was running the opposite way, toward the woods. Roy knew he had to find out what this kid was up to so he followed his trail into the mango groves and found a campsite. Roy was just plain nosy and couldn't resist picking up the black trash bag next to a sleeping bag. But when the contents began to wriggle and move he wished he hadn't been so inquisitive. Roy dumped it back on the ground only to find himself standing in a swarming mass of water moccasins. Even though the deadly snakes terrified him, he couldn't help but notice that their tails sparkled with glitter. Who decorates snakes, especially poisonous ones? What was this kid up to and how was Roy going to get out of the mess he had just gotten himself into?

Excerpt: Page 13, first paragraph, through end of fourth paragraph on page 16.

Curriculum Connection: Science
As the Everglades are being filled in for houses and other types of buildings, animals are losing their habitat. Have students use library media center resources to research the animals that live in the Florida Everglades and face extinction due to man's encroachment on their homes. Have students suggest ways to ensure that these animals do not become extinct.

Similar Titles:

George, Jean Craighead, **Case of the Missing Cutthroats.** The Ecological Mystery Series. HarperTrophy, 1999, 160pp. $5.99. ISBN: 0064406474.

George, Jean Craighead, **There's an Owl in the Shower.** HarperCollins, 1995, 133pp. $14.89. ISBN: 0060248920. HarperTrophy, 1997, 144pp. $5.99. ISBN: 0064406822. Recorded Books, 2000. $35.20. ISBN: 0788741837.

Hobbs, Will, **The Maze.** HarperCollins, 1998, 208pp. $15.99. ISBN: 0688150926. HarperTrophy, 1999, 206pp. $5.99. ISBN: 038072913X. Recorded Books, 1999. $37.00. ISBN: 0788738925.

Skurzynski, Gloria, **Hunted.** The Mysteries in Our National Parks Series. National Geographic, 2000, 147pp. $15.95. ISBN: 0792270533. National Geographic, 2001, 160pp. $5.95. ISBN: 0792276655.

Smith, Roland, **Jaguar.** Hyperion, 1997, 192pp. $15.89. ISBN: 0786802260. Hyperion, 1998, 256pp. $5.95. ISBN: 0786813121. Recorded Books, 1999. $38.00. ISBN: 0788738283.

Hobbs, Will, *Wild Man Island.*

HarperCollins, 2002, 184pp. $16.89. ISBN: 0060298103. HarperCollins, 2003, 184pp. $5.99. ISBN: 0380733102. Recorded Books, 2002. $28.00. ISBN: 1402522746.

Web Site: <www.willhobbsauthor.com>
Subjects: Dogs, Fathers and Sons, Grieving, Survival
Genres: Adventure, Mystery
Levels: BL 7-10, K 5-8, SLJ 5-9

Annotation: Fourteen-year-old Andy Galloway is stranded when he sneaks away from his kayaking group in Southeast Alaska to visit Admiralty Island, the remote location where his father died, and comes face to face with a hermit who is living on the island.

Booktalk: It's freezing cold and raining when Andy Galloway is literally spit out of the raging sea onto Admiralty Island in a remote area of Southeast Alaska. Andy had snuck away from his guided kayaking tour to make the supposedly easy two-mile crossing to Admiralty when a storm raged into the strait and stranded him on the island with no food and no shelter. His goal had been to visit the place his archeologist father died nine years before while searching for remnants of prehistoric immigrants to America. Now Andy's goal is to stay alive. Although he is shivering and shaking from the cold, Andy is sure he isn't hallucinating when he sees the legendary Wild Man of Admiralty Island running through the woods. It has to be him – who else would be dressed in clothes made of bark, with a scraggly beard and long hair that looks like it hasn't been cut or combed in years? Maybe he's the link his father was looking for. Andy is about to find out.

Excerpt: Page 56 through the third paragraph on page 59.

Curriculum Connection: Science
Have students use library media center resources to determine Admiralty Island's location, climate, and the types of plants that grow on the island that could help keep someone alive who is stranded there. Have them make a list of the plants Andy can safely eat.

Similar Titles:
Clements, Andrew, *A Week in the Woods.* Simon & Schuster, 2002, 160pp. $16.95. ISBN 068982596X. Aladdin, 2004, 208pp. $5.99. ISBN: 0689858027. Random House Audio, 2002. $25.00. ISBN: 0807209619.
George, Jean Craighead, *Julie of the Wolves.* HarperCollins, 1972, 192pp. $16.95. ISBN: 0060219440. HarperCollins, 2003, 176pp. $5.99. ISBN: 0060540958. Recorded Books, 2000. $39.00. CD. ISBN: 0788734490.
Mikaelsen, Ben, *Touching Spirit Bear.* HarperCollins, 2001, 256pp. $16.89. ISBN: 0060291494. HarperTrophy, 2002, 256pp. $5.99. ISBN: 038080560X. Random House Audio, 2001. $25.00. ISBN: 0807204455.

Paulsen, Gary, ***Hatchet.*** Atheneum, 2000, 208pp. $16.95. ISBN: 0689840926. Simon & Schuster, 1999, 289pp. $5.99. ISBN: 0689826990. Random House Audio, 1992. $25.00. ISBN: 0553470876. Random House Audio, 2004. $14.99. CD. ISBN: 0807204773. Speare, Elizabeth George, ***Sign of the Beaver.*** Houghton Mifflin, 1983, 135pp. $16.00. ISBN: 0395338905. Yearling, 1994, 144pp. $5.99. ISBN: 0440479002. Random House Audio, 2000. $18.00. ISBN: 0807279757. Random House Audio, 2004. $14.99. CD. ISBN: 1400084970.

42 Holm, Jennifer L., ***Boston Jane: The Claim.***

The Boston Jane Series. HarperCollins, 2004, 229pp. $16.89. ISBN: 0060290463. HarperTrophy, 2005, 240pp. $5.99. ISBN: 0064408825.

Web Site: <www.jenniferholm.com>
Subjects: Cooking, Frontier and Pioneer Life, Native Americans, Orphans, Relationships, Self-Esteem
Genre: Historical, Multicultural
Levels: BL 5-8, K 5-9, SLJ 6 up

Annotation: During the 1850s, 17-year-old Jane Peck makes her home in Shoalwater Bay, a settlement in the Washington Territory, and is adjusting to the frontier lifestyle nicely until her childhood nemesis arrives and tries to ruin Jane's reputation with her fiancé and friends.

Booktalk: Jane Peck, the feisty young woman who followed her heart to an isolated fishing village in the Washington Territory, only to be abandoned by the man she was to marry, is now impatiently waiting for her very own home – a wonderful house that is being built by the new man in her life. The site of her future home, on her very own land claim, is where Jane runs to when she sees her childhood nemesis, Sally Biddle, and her family getting off the ship in Shoalwater Bay. From the looks of the piles of luggage accompanying them they aren't here for just a visit. Sally Biddle had made Jane's younger years miserable. Why did she have to appear now, when things are going so well with the other women in Shoalwater Bay and with Jehu? Jane has good reason to be upset by Sally's appearance. You see, Sally Biddle's father is in cahoots with that low-down no-good man who left Jane alone in the wilderness when she arrived in the Washington Territory. The two men plan on using a legal technicality to take Jane's land away from her. And Sally isn't through with ruining Jane's life either. Not by any means. Sally intends to make Jehu fall for her instead of Jane and will use any type of deception needed to do so.

Excerpt: Page 1 through third full paragraph on page 2.

Curriculum Connection: Social Studies
Have students use library media center resources to research the Chinook Indians and the government's attempt to relocate them onto reservations during the 1800s.

Have students discuss the crucial role the Chinooks played in helping white settlers survive the hostile northwest coast climate.

Similar Titles:

Hobbs, Will, ***Ghost Canoe.*** HarperCollins, 1997, 208pp. $16.99. ISBN: 0688141935. HarperTrophy, 1998, 208pp. $5.99. ISBN: 0380725371. Random House Audio, 2004. $32.00. ISBN: 0807204498. Random House Audio, 2004, $38.00. CD. ISBN: 0807204501.

Holm, Jennifer L., ***Boston Jane: An Adventure.*** The Boston Jane Series. HarperCollins, 2001, 288pp. $17.89. ISBN: 0060287389X. HarperTrophy, 2002, 288pp. $6.99. ISBN: 0064408493.

Holm, Jennifer L., ***Boston Jane: Wilderness Days.*** The Boston Jane Series. HarperCollins, 2002, 244pp. $16.99. ISBN: 0060290439. HarperTrophy, 2004, 256pp. $5.99. ISBN: 0064408817.

MacDonald, Margaret Reed, ***Ghost Stories of the Pacific Northwest.*** August House, 1995, 256pp. $24.95. ISBN: 0874834368. August House, 1995, 256pp. $14.95. ISBN: 0874834376.

Ringstad, Muriel, ***Eye of the Changer: Northwest Indian Tale.*** Alaska Northwest Books, 1984, 96pp. $9.95. ISBN: 088240251X.

43

Holm, Jennifer L., *The Creek.*

HarperCollins, 2003, 232pp. $16.89. ISBN: 0060001348. HarperCollins, 2004, 304pp. $5.99. ISBN: 0060001356.

Web Site: <www.jenniferholm.com>
Subjects: Accidents, Crime, Death, Friendship, Mental Illness, Murder
Genres: Mystery, Realistic
Levels: BL, 6-8, K 5-9, PW 7 up

Annotation: During the summer of Penny Carson's 13th year Caleb Devlin returns home after spending years in a juvenile facility for killing a child in their quiet suburban Philadelphia neighborhood. Caleb is the main suspect in another child's death but Penny knows Caleb is innocent and puts herself in danger when she discovers that the killer is one of the new neighborhood boys.

Booktalk: The neighborhood is abuzz with talk about Caleb Delvin being back home. Penny has heard all the stories about him but she wasn't living in the neighborhood when he tortured neighbors' pets and killed a young child. But Penny does know that Caleb is hanging out by the Creek again because he stopped her when she was dumb enough to go to the Creek by herself. She thought he would hurt her bad, but he just scared her bad and thought it was really funny. Caleb is still one bad kid and when pets begin to disappear everyone suspects Caleb, even Penny. But, when another murder occurs, Penny knows Caleb couldn't have killed that little girl. Penny knows something about Caleb that no one else does. She learned it at the Creek.

Excerpt: Page 38.

Curriculum Connection: Health

Penny experiences panic attacks when she is scared and cannot breathe. Have students use library media center resources to research what happens to the body during a panic attack and why breathing into a paper bag helps a person stop hyperventilating.

Similar Titles:

Hahn, Mary Downing, ***Dead Man in Indian Creek.*** Clarion, 1990, 144pp. $15.00. ISBN: 0395523974. HarperTrophy, 1991, 144pp. $5.99. ISBN: 0380713624.

L'Engle, Madeleine, ***Troubling a Star.*** Farrar, Straus & Giroux, 1994, 304pp. $19.00. ISBN: 0374377839. Bantam Doubleday Dell, 1995, 296pp. $5.99. ISBN: 0440219507.

Roberts, Willo Davis, ***Scared Stiff.*** Simon & Schuster, 2001, 192pp. $4.99. ISBN: 0689846894.

Sachar, Louis, ***Holes.*** Farrar, Straus & Giroux, 1998, 233pp. $17.00. ISBN: 0374332657. Yearling, 2000, 240pp. $6.50. ISBN: 0440414806. Random House Audio, 2000. $25.00. ISBN: 080728162X. Random House Audio, 2001. $28.00. CD. ISBN: 0807262021.

Van Draanen, Wendelin, ***Sammy Keyes and the Search for Snake Eyes.*** The Sammy Keyes Series. Knopf, 2002, 277pp. $15.95. ISBN: 0375811753. Random House, 2003, 288pp. $5.50. ISBN: 044041900X. Live Oak Media, 2003. $31.95. ISBN: 1591122740. Live Oak Media, 2004. $41.95. CD. ISBN: 1591122805.

44 Holt, Kimberly Willis, *My Louisiana Sky.*

Holt, 1998, 200pp. $15.95. ISBN: 0805052518. Yearling, 2000, 208pp. $5.99. ISBN: 0440415705. Random House, 2004. $30.00. ISBN: 0807282898.

Web Site: <www.kimberlyholt.com>
Subjects: Death, Disabilities, Family Problems, Friendship, Grandmothers, Mothers and Daughters, Prejudices, Self-Identity
Genres: Historical
Lists: 1999 BBYA, 1999 CN, 2000 YAC
Levels: BL 6-9, K 5-9, PW 4-7, SLJ 6-8, V 6-9

Annotation: After the death of her grandmother in rural 1950s Louisiana, 12-year-old Tiger Ann realizes that, rather than going to live with her aunt in the city, she wants to stay at home and take care of her mentally handicapped parents.

Booktalk: Tiger Ann loved having a mom who played with her. The other kids' mothers were too busy cleaning house and other grown up stuff to spend time outside playing with their daughters. That was not the case with Tiger's mom. She loved to play and watch TV as much as Tiger did, maybe even more. Granny had told Tiger that her Momma was different from most mothers and Tiger Ann was glad. That is until she started to get a bit older and cared what the other girls, and Jesse Wade, thought about her. It was the day that Tiger Ann took her mother to the book mobile that she first felt embarrassed by her mother's childlike behavior. Tiger had left her mother busy looking at picture books in the book mobile and wandered into the gymnasium. There was the group of girls that Tiger wanted to be friends with, but they stopped talking and just stared at her when she came in. Before she could get up the courage to go talk to them her mother came rushing in, crying Tiger's name at the top of her lungs. She was scared that Tiger had left her behind. Tiger Ann's mother was waving about her checked out copy of *The Little Engine that Could* – a book that Tiger Ann and everyone else in the gymnasium knew was about all her mother was able to read. Tiger Ann was abruptly aware that she was now "older" than her very own Momma.

Excerpt: Page 54, second paragraph, through page 59.

Curriculum Connection: Health
Have students use library media center resources to research different types of learning disabilities before brainstorming as a group how they would interact with and help family members if they had learning problems similar to Tiger Ann's mother and father.

Similar Titles:
Byars, Betsy, ***Summer of the Swans.*** Viking, 1971, 142pp. $15.99. ISBN: 0670681903. Penguin Putnam, 2004, 144pp. $5.99. ISBN: 0142401145. Recorded Books, 1997. $19.00. ISBN: 0788703838. Recorded Books, 2000. $29.00. CD. ISBN: 0788746537.
Matthews, Kezi, ***John Riley's Daughter.*** Cricket, 2000, 144pp. $15.95. ISBN: 081262775X. Penguin, 2002, 128pp. $5.99. ISBN: 0142302120.
Meyer, Donald J., ***Views from Our Shoes: Growing Up with a Brother or Sister with Special Needs.*** Woodbine House, 1997, 114pp. $14.95. ISBN: 0933149980.
Shyer, Marlene Fanta, ***Welcome Home, Jellybean.*** Aladdin, 1988, 160pp. $4.99. ISBN 0689712138.
Tashjian, Janet, ***Tru Confessions.*** Holt, 1997, 161pp. $15.95. ISBN: 0805052542. Scholastic, 1999, 167pp. $4.99. ISBN: 0590960474.

45 Hooper, Mary, *Petals in the Ashes.*
Bloomsbury, 2004, 192pp. $16.95. ISBN: 1582349363.

Web Site: <www.maryhooper.co.uk>
Subjects: Cooking, Death, Fires, Illness, Infants, Sisters
Genres: Historical, International
Levels: BL 5-8, K 6-8, SLJ 6-10

Annotation: London sweet shop owners Hannah and Sarah leave plague-ridden London to take an orphaned baby girl to her aunt, only to be forced into a filthy pestilence house until all three are declared free of the plague. Hannah returns to London with her younger sister Anne to reopen the sweets shops just before the Great Fire of 1666 begins.

Booktalk: Hannah and Sarah are thoroughly exhausted after their escape from London with orphaned baby Grace. They are so relieved that they escaped dying from the plague that they want nothing more than to curl up in a clean warm bed. Of course Lady Jane of Dorchester, baby Grace's aunt, will welcome them with open arms and escort them to rooms with downy soft beds. Sarah is sure she can sleep for a week. After being bounced about in the carriage until their bones ached, the sisters pull up in front of the grand front entrance. A woman dressed in black runs toward them, but she gasps in horror and backs away as soon as she hears that they are from London. Before either girl can tell her why they are there, the woman runs back into the house and closes the door. It seems like hours before Lady Jane appears, with a posy of flowers in front of her nose, sniffing at the flowers the entire time she speaks to them. Even though they tell Lady Jane that her sister has died, she shouts, "No! Get back!" when they try to give her baby Grace. It is clear that this woman would have liked to turn her back on all three of them, but she cannot because the baby girl is her niece. So instead Lady Jane sends them to a pestilence house – a place where more die from the plague than survive it. The helpful sisters certainly didn't receive the open armed welcome they expected from baby Grace's family. So what do they do now?

Excerpt: Pages 78 through 80.

Curriculum Connection: Social Studies
The "Notes on the Great Fire of London" state that Robert Hubert confessed to starting the fire. Have students use library media center resources to research the various theories of how the fire started, choosing the theory they most agree with and supporting their choice with research documentation.

Similar Titles:
Hooper, Mary, *At the Sign of the Sugared Plum.* Bloomsbury, 2003, 200pp. ISBN: 1582348499.

Oldfield, Pamela, ***The Great Plague: The Diary of Alice Payton, London 1665-1666.*** The My Story Series. Scholastic, 2004, 192pp. $10.95. ISBN: 0439992281.
Prince, Maggie, ***House on Hound Hill.*** Houghton Mifflin, 1998, 242pp. $16.00. ISBN: 0395907020. Houghton Mifflin, 2003, 256pp. $6.95. ISBN: 0618331247.
Pullman, Phillip, ***The Ruby in the Smoke.*** Random House, 1988, 230pp. $6.50. ISBN: 0394895894. Random House Audio, 2004. $26.00. ISBN: 140008511X.
Shields, Charles J., ***Plague and Fire of London.*** Chelsea, 2001, 120pp. $21.95. ISBN: 0791063240.

Jarvis, Robin, *The Final Reckoning.*

The Deptford Mice Trilogy. Chronicle, 2002, 304pp. $17.95. ISBN: 1587171929. Chronicle, 2003, 304pp. $6.95. ISBN: 1587172445.

Web Site: <www.robinjarvis.com>
Subjects: Animals, Cats, Ghosts, Magic, Mice, Rats, Survival, Violence
Genres: Fantasy, Horror, , International, Supernatural
Levels: BL 5-8, SLJ 6-8, V 6-9

Annotation: The mice and bats of London battle the evil ghost cat Jupiter and his army of rats to save the earth from an eternal deadly cold blackness in the third book of the Deptford Mice Trilogy.

Booktalk: Have you ever been so cold that it felt like you would batter your teeth right down to the stubs from their chattering? Or that your fingers and toes were so cold that you couldn't feel them anymore and that they would fall right off? But as cold as you were you knew, eventually, you would be warm again. You would go inside, or the weather would warm up, and so would your body. But, what if there was no end to the cold and winter was never going to end? In the final installment of the Deptford Mice Trilogy, that is exactly what is about to happen – eternal winter. It will be the deep freeze for everyone. The mice have long since burnt all of the furniture and other wood they can find so they know their little ones will soon freeze to death. If that isn't bad enough, they learned that a marauding band of rats is on the loose and these vicious rats love to chew on tender little mice ears before they swallow the mouse whole. Leading them is the evil ghost cat Jupiter, once the lord of the rats of the sewers. The mice thought Jupiter was dead. Well, he still is kind of dead, but just barely. The rats are about to bring the ghost cat back to life and if the mice can't stop Jupiter's resurrection the world as they know it will come to an end.

Excerpt: Pages 8 through 12.

Curriculum Connection: Science

Have students use library media center resources to research the climactic changes that would have to take place for an "eternal winter" to occur on earth. Have them debate whether or not something similar has or could ever happen.

Similar Titles:

Barker, Clive, ***Abarat.*** HarperCollins, 2002, 432pp. $26.89. ISBN: 0060510846. HarperCollins, 2003, 432pp. $11.99. ISBN: 0064407330. HarperCollins Audio, 2002. $39.95. ISBN: 0060510757.

Jacques, Brian, ***Martin the Warrior.*** The Redwall Series. Philomel, 1994, 376pp. $23.99. ISBN: 0399226702. Penguin, 2004, 376pp. $7.99. ISBN: 0142400556. Random House Audio, 1999. $35.00. ISBN: 0807281824.

Jarvis, Robin, ***The Crystal Prison.*** The Deptford Mice Trilogy. Chronicle, 2001, 250pp. $17.95. ISBN: 1587171074. Chronicle, 2002, 256pp. $6.95. ISBN: 1587171619.

Jarvis, Robin, ***The Dark Portal.*** The Deptford Mice Trilogy. Chronicle, 2000, 241pp. $17.95. ISBN: 587170213. Chronicle, 2001, 256pp. $6.95. ISBN: 1587171120. Blackstone Audio Books, 2002. $44.95. ISBN: 0786123311. Blackstone Audio Books, 2002. $56.00. CD. ISBN: 0786193476.

O'Brien, Robert C. ***Mrs. Frisby and the Rats of NIMH.*** Atheneum, 1971, 240pp. $18.00. ISBN: 0689206518. Aladdin, 1986, 240pp. $5.50. ISBN: 0689710682.

47 Jarvis, Robin, *The Thorn Ogres of Hagwood.*

The Hagwood Trilogy. Harcourt, 2002, 256pp. $16.00. ISBN: 0152167528. Harcourt, 2004, 264pp. $5.95. ISBN: 0152051228.

Web Site: <www.robinjarvis.com>
Subjects: Brothers and Sisters, Magic, Self-Esteem, Violence, Witchcraft
Genres: Fantasy
Level: BL 5-8, K 5-10, PW 5 up, SLJ 5-7, V 6-9

Annotation: When a young shape shifting werling evokes the attention and ire of the High Queen of the Hollow Hill she sends her Thorn Ogres into the werling village to find him. After a furious battle on the ground and in the trees, the feisty werlings defeat the Thorn Ogres.

Booktalk: Okay, so I am not so good at this. No matter how much I sniff the skins of animals it takes me forever to shape shift into one of them, and sometimes not all of me shifts. And the other werlings laugh at me when that happens – especially my snotty older sister. She is such a pain! And, look at Finnan over there. He is one of the best shape shifters in the upper classmen group. I know I will never be as good as him, but at least I didn't bring the wrath of the Queen of the Hollow Hills down on us. What did Finnan think he was doing by taking us into the forest – a bunch of young werlings barely able to shift? If it weren't for the Smith, we'd never have made it back to the village. But, something is bothering me about that Smith. There has to be a reason he isn't with the fairy court anymore. Something just isn't right about him. I have a very bad feeling that we werlings are not the forgotten folk of the forest anymore. But, I don't know what I'm more afraid of – the attention of the High Queen's Thorn Ogres or being caught by Frighty Aggie. I used to think Frighty Aggie was just a story the elders told the little ones to keep them out of the forest, but now I know different after Finnan took us into the forest. What was that noise I heard? Did you hear something?

Excerpt: Page 52 through paragraph six on page 55.

Curriculum Connections: Art, Language Arts, Science

The werlings have the ability to shape shift into animals about the same size as themselves, but to do so they have to know the ways of that animal. Have students use library resources to research an animal similar in size to themselves that they would like to shape shift into. Based on what they learned about the animal and how it lives, have students draw a series of pictures of themselves in the shape shifting process. The pictures should be accompanied by a narrative of how it felt to become that animal and how they spent a day as that animal – what they ate, where they slept, etc.

Similar Titles:

Collins, Suzanne, ***Gregor the Overlander and the Prophecy of Bane.*** Scholastic, 2004, 312pp. $16.95. ISBN: 0439650755. Scholastic, 2005, 304pp. $6.99. ISBN: 0439650763.

DiCamillo, Kate, ***Tale of Despereaux: Being the Story of a Mouse, a Princess, Some Soup, and a Spool of Thread.*** Candlewick, 2003, 273pp. $17.99. ISBN: 0763617229. Random House Audio, 2003. $25.00. ISBN: 0807219479. Random House Audio, 2005. $14.99. CD. ISBN: 1400099137.

Hunter, Erin, ***Into the Wild.*** The Warriors Series. HarperCollins, 2003, 272pp. $15.99. ISBN: 0060000023. HarperCollins, 2004, 288pp. $5.99. ISBN: 0060525509.

Lasky, Kathryn, ***The Capture.*** The Guardians of Ga'Hoole Series. Scholastic, 2003, 226pp. $4.99. ISBN: 0439405572.

Vornholt, John, ***The Troll King.*** Thomson Gale, 2003, 272pp. $22.95. ISBN: 0786250496. Simon & Schuster, 2002, 216pp. $4.99. ISBN: 0743424123.

48 Jinks, Catherine, *Pagan's Vows.*

The Pagan Chronicles. Candlewick, 2004, 330pp. $16.99. ISBN: 0763620211.

Subjects: Crime, Emotional Problems, Friendship, Knights and Knighthood, Middle Ages, Orphans, Religion, Teachers
Genres: Historical, International, Multicultural, Mystery
Levels: BL 8-10, K 7-10, SLJ 7-9

Annotation: Seventeen-year-old Arab born Pagan Kidrouk joins Lord Roland in a 12th-century French monastery. Roland is seeking solace from the horrors of the Crusades, but wisecracking Pagan gets himself in trouble with the Brothers as he tries to discover why and who is embezzling money from the monastery coffers.

Booktalk: I would follow Lord Roland anywhere, but why did he have to choose a monastery? I grew up in one of these dismal places and have no desire to be back in one. They make you wear a dress and they shave the top of your head so it always feels cold. And I do not find it the least bit funny when the monk who does the shaving has to make fun about the fact that even though I am 17 there is no reason to shave my face. Roland is quite content to pray and keep the vow of silence. Being silent is not easy for me, not even during our boring lessons. Master Clement does not appreciate the fact that I am somewhat of an authority on Latin grammar. It was just one little comment, well maybe it was a correction rather than a comment, but that was no reason for him to stick me with Boethius. No, Boethius isn't a person, at least not anymore – he's dead – and I am going to die from carrying his book around with me. It is practically bigger than I am. But, then I realized Boethius is actually quite a good friend. I just conveniently "lose" him and when I tell this to Master Clement as we are about to sit down for yet another Latin lesson he gets furious and sends me off to find the wayward Boethius. While I am searching for the "lost" book I have a few minutes to search the monastery for clues as to who is benefiting from the high count of how many beggars are given money each day. With a little help from the wayward Boethius I may just find out who is getting rich from the money that should be going to the beggars.

Excerpt: Page 12 through first three lines on page 17.

Curriculum Connection: Social Studies
Have students use library media center resources to research the role monasteries played in the recovery of soldiers returning the Crusades. Have them discuss how this role differed after the Crusades versus before the Crusades.

Similar Titles:
Cadnum, Michael, ***The Leopard Sword.*** Viking, 2002, 224pp. $15.99. ISBN: 0670899089.
Cushman, Karen, ***Catherine, Called Birdy.*** Houghton Mifflin, 1994, 176pp. $16.00. ISBN: 0395681863. HarperCollins, 1995, 224pp. $6.50. ISBN: 0064405842.

Cushman, Karen. ***Matilda Bone.*** Clarion, 2000, 167pp. $15.00. ISBN: 0395881560. Yearling, 2002, 176pp. $5.00. ISBN: 0440418224. Random House Audio, 2004. $30.00. ISBN: 0807287377.

Jinks, Catherine, ***Pagan in Exile.*** The Pagan Chronicles. Candlewick, 2004, 326pp. $15.99. ISBN: 0763620203. Candlewick, 2005, 336pp. $6.99. ISBN: 0763626910.

Jinks, Catherine, ***Pagan's Crusade.*** The Pagan Chronicles. Candlewick, 2003, 256pp. $15.99. ISBN: 076362019X. Candlewick, 2004, 256pp. $6.99. ISBN: 0763625841.

Kerr, M.E., *Snakes Don't Miss Their Mothers.* — 49

HarperCollins, 2003, 194pp. $16.89. ISBN: 0060526254.

Web Site: <www.mekerr.com>
Subjects: Animals, Cats, Dogs, Fathers and Daughters, Grieving, Holidays, Pets
Genres: Fantasy
Levels: BL 4-6, PW 3-7, SLJ 3-6, V 5-7

Annotation: The animals at Critters animal shelter in the Hamptons narrate their need for love and attention and their hope that a family will adopt them by Christmas. Human characters include a 12-year-old actress and the shelter director's son.

Booktalk: I listened to Mrs. Splinter, the director, asking lots of questions of the tall skinny guy she called Mr. Twilight. I hear this conversation often about Placido. He gets adopted a lot, but it is just a matter of days before he shows back up. You see, Placido has a major attitude. It probably has something to do with the fact that he has only one eye and no front claws. Whatever you do, don't ask him how he lost that eye! Living in an animal shelter is quite a blow for a male Siamese who once was a pampered show cat. I'm used to it – I have been here a long time. I cross my paws for luck when I say goodbye to Placido as he is carried by me in the pet carrier. I really hope he does well with Mr. Twilight's daughter. I heard him say that she lost her mother so this girl knows what is it like to be alone. Maybe Placido will get it right this time. One of us should be out of here and in a home for Christmas.

Excerpt: Page 58, last paragraph, through second paragraph on page 60.

Curriculum Connection: Science
Along with the dogs and cats at Critters, there are exotic pets. Have students use library media center resources to select and research an exotic pet and how to care for it.

Similar Titles:
Baglio, Ben M., ***Owl in the Office.*** The Animal Ark Series. Apple, 1999, 192pp. $3.99. ISBN: 0439084164.

George, Jean Craighead, ***Frightful's Mountain.*** Penguin Putnam, 1999, 176pp. $15.99. ISBN: 0525461663. Penguin, 2001, 272pp. $5.99. ISBN: 0141312351. Recorded Books, 2001. $52.00. ISBN: 0788745530. Recorded Books, 2001. $58.00. CD. ISBN: 0788752189.

Kehret, Peg, ***Shelter Dogs: Amazing Stories of Adopted Strays.*** Whitman, 1999, 136pp. $14.95. ISBN: 0807573345. Whitman, 2004, 144pp. $5.95. ISBN: 0807573361.

North, Sterling, ***Rascal.*** Penguin, 1984, 189pp. $16.99. ISBN: 0525188398. Penguin, 1990, 189pp. $5.99. ISBN: 0140344454. Random House Audio, 2002. $25.00. ISBN: 0807209562. Recorded Books, 2000. $36.00. ISBN: 0788742124.

Sidman, Joyce, ***The World According to Dog: Poems and Teen Voices.*** Houghton Mifflin, 2003, 80pp. $15.00. ISBN: 0618174974.

50 Lowry, Lois, *Gathering Blue.*

Houghton Mifflin, 2000, 215pp. $15.00. ISBN: 618055819. Laurel Leaf, 2002, 240pp. $6.50. ISBN: 0440229499. Random House Audio, 2000. $25.00. ISBN: 0807261505.

Web Site: <www.loislowry.com>
Subject: Disabilities, Grieving, Occupations, Orphans, Self-Identity
Genres: Science Fiction
Lists: 2002 YAC
Levels: K 6-8, PW 5 up, SLJ 5-9, V 7-12

Annotation: In a futuristic world, Kira discovers her talent is to embroider pictures onto the Singer's robe, scenes that tell the story of their world. Kira's needlework skills keep her alive in a world where handicapped individuals are normally abandoned at birth.

Booktalk: Kira knew her mother wouldn't reply, but she had to ask one more time, "Mother?" No reply. Kira had not expected one. It had been four days since Kira's mother died and by now the last of her spirit had drifted away. Adult spirits always took four days to leave the body. Kira looked around her – there were other people in the Field of Leaving tending the spirits of their loved ones who have died. There was a young mother with her infant. But she wouldn't have to stay in this horrible place for four days; infant spirits didn't take that long to leave the body. Kira knew it was time to leave, but she couldn't bear the thought of what would happen next. The Diggers would throw a thin layer of soil over her mother, but at night the savage creatures would come and destroy her body. Kira couldn't bear to think of her mother's bones scattered about the Field of Leaving. Kira slowly got to her feet and reached for her walking stick, but then she realized she had nowhere to go. Their cottage had been burned to the ground because of her mother's sickness. Not knowing what would happen to her now, Kira limped toward the village. As Kira slowly walked toward an uncertain future she remembered her mother's tale of how they had come to take Kira to the Field right after she was born. In their society an infant with a twisted leg was not fit to live. It had to quickly be given back to the earth before it became human. But her mother convinced them that Kira had something to offer. She said that you could tell from the brilliance of Kira's eyes and her long shapely fingers that Kira would not be a burden. With her mother's protection gone, it was now time for the skill of those long shapely fingers to keep Kira alive.

Excerpt: Page 4, first paragraph, through page 8.

Curricular Connection: Science
Kira was taught how to make dye from plants, tree bark, and other natural ingredients. Have students use library media center resources to research natural dyes and, using pieces of white cotton, create their own naturally colored squares that can be made into a classroom quilt or pillows.

Similar Titles:
Haddix, Margaret Peterson, **Among the Hidden.** The Shadow Children Series. Simon & Schuster, 1998, 160pp. $16.95. ISBN: 0689817002. Aladdin, 2000, 160pp. $5.99. ISBN: 0689824750.
Hautman, Pete, **Hole in the Sky.** Simon & Schuster, 2001, 192pp. $16.00. ISBN: 0689831188.
Lowry, Lois, **The Giver.** Houghton Mifflin, 1993, 192pp. $16.00. ISBN: 0395645662. Bantam, 1999, 192pp. $6.99. ISBN: 0553571338. Random House Audio, 1995. $26.00. ISBN: 055347359X. Random House Audio, 2001. $28.00. CD. ISBN: 080726203X.
Lowry, Lois, **The Messenger.** Houghton Mifflin, 2004, 176pp. $16.00. ISBN: 0618404414. Random House Audio, 2004. $25.00. ISBN: 0807223727. Random House Audio, 2004. $30.00. CD. ISBN: 1400086205.
Pullman, Phillip, **The Golden Compass.** His Dark Materials Series. Knopf, 1996, 416pp. $20.00. ISBN: 0679879242. Dell, 2003, 368pp. $6.99. ISBN: 0440238137. Random House Audio, 1999. $37.00. ISBN: 0807281808. Random House Audio, 2004. $44.00. CD. ISBN: 0807204714.

51 Lynch, Chris, *The Gravedigger's Cottage.*
HarperCollins, 2004, 199pp. $16.89. ISBN: 0066239419.

Subjects: Accidents, Animals, Brothers and Sisters, Death, Emotional Problems, Fathers and Daughters, Grieving, Moving, Pets
Genres: Realistic
Levels: BL 6-9, K 5-8, PW 7 up, SLJ 7 up, V 7-12

Annotation: Fourteen-year-old Sylvia and ten-year-old Walter move to a New England seaside cottage with their grieving father. They leave behind two deceased mothers and a backyard pet cemetery. Chapters alternate between the descriptions of how the pets died with Sylvia's narrative of the family settling into their new home and their father's unsettling behavior.

Booktalk: Sylvia, certainly not Sylvie, and Vee to only her dad and brother in the most intimate of moments, is the glue that keeps this family together. But, things are not going very well at the moment – the family is coming apart at the seams. It doesn't help any that the seaside cottage their father has purchased, so they can get away from the bad memories and the ever-growing pet cemetery in the yard of their old house, is called the Gravedigger's Cottage. And now she and her little brother Walter are being called the DiggerKids and their dad has become the Gravedigger to everyone in the nearby village. Sylvia would never admit it to herself, but perhaps that is a fitting name for her dad at the moment. He won't go back to work and now he says the house must be sealed of all leakage. One day she finds him on his hands and knees in the dirty old cellar trying to fill in gaps on the dirt floor and cement walls with plaster repair paste. He is covered in dust and has a wild look in his eyes. It is quite some time before Sylvia can convince him to leave the basement. And Sylvia really doesn't want to discuss the rat, which she is sure is imaginary, that her dad keeps saying he sees. Right now Sylvia is worried about her dad's state of mind and him carrying on about an imaginary rat isn't helping any.

Excerpt: Page 4, beginning after the break, to break at top of page 6.

Curriculum Connection: Social Studies
Have students use library media center resources and public library resources to research the historic houses in their area to discover how they got their names. Have them share stories they have heard about the houses, or other buildings in the area.

Similar Titles:
Bode, N.E., *Anybodies.* HarperCollins, 2004, 288pp. $15.99. ISBN: 0060557354.
Horvath, Polly, *Everything on a Waffle.* Farrar, Straus & Giroux, 2001, 160pp. $16.00. ISBN: 0374322368. Farrar, Straus & Giroux, 2004, 160pp. $5.95. ISBN: 0374422087.

Ives, David, ***Monsieur Eek.*** HarperCollins, 2001, 192pp. $15.89. ISBN: 0060295307. HarperTrophy, 2003, 192pp. $5.99. ISBN: 0064473015.

Martin, Ann M., ***A Corner of the Universe.*** Scholastic, 2002, 208pp. $15.95. ISBN: 0439388805. Scholastic, 2003, 189pp. $5.99. ISBN: 0439388813. Random House Audio, 2004. $30.00. ISBN: 0807216712. Random House Audio, 2004 $35.00. CD. ISBN: 080721776X.

Peck, Richard, ***A Year Down Yonder.*** Dial, 2000, 130pp. $16.99. ISBN: 0803725183. Penguin, 2002, 144pp. $5.99. ISBN: 0142300705. Random House Audio, 2000. $18.00. ISBN: 080726167X. Random House Audio, 2004. $14.99. CD. ISBN: 1400084962.

Martin, Ann M., *Here Today.*

Scholastic, 2004, 308pp. $16.95. ISBN: 0439579449. Random House Audio, 2004. $26.00. ISBN: 140009044X.

Subjects: Bullies, Elderly, Family Problems, Friendship, Mothers and Daughters, Prejudices, Schools
Genre: Historical
Levels: BL 5-7, K 5-7, PW 5-9, SLJ 4-8

Annotation: Eleven-year-old Ellie, a target for the sixth grade bullies, knows that the assassination of President Kennedy has thrown her already unstable mother over the edge. She is no longer satisfied with being Spectacle, New York's beauty queen and leaves to pursue her unrealistic dream of becoming a famous actress.

Booktalk: Bad things have happened on Witch Tree Lane as long as Ellie can remember. The families who live there try to ignore the way they are treated, but they realize that the level of harassment is escalating beyond smashed mailboxes and witches painted on trees. Bad things are happening on the bus and at school too. It's because all the kids who live on Witch Tree Lane are misfits. When they get on the bus the other kids move away from them like they have cooties or something. Ellie knows that they are a motley lot, but calling Albert a dirty Hebe and making fun of Etienne and Dominique because their hair looks like it hasn't been washed in weeks is difficult for Ellie to ignore. Ellie decides she has had enough when Tammy, the new girl in class, calls her to say that everyone in their class is going to slam Holly. Holly is a Witch Tree Lane kid and Ellie's best friend. Ellie refuses to join in slamming Holly, knowing full well that she will be slammed too. For the next few days Holly and Ellie are slammed against lockers, slammed into walls, and slammed onto the floor. But, being covered with bruises and cuts, as well as getting in trouble at home for their ripped clothes, was easier for Holly and Ellie to tolerate than what comes next. Tammy and her friends aren't through with them yet.

Excerpt: Page 13 to break on page 17.

Curriculum Connection: Social Studies
The teachers and students in Ellie's school are in shock when they hear President Kennedy has been shot. Have students use library media center resources to research the media's coverage of the first few days after the assassination as well as interview their grandparents as to their memories of that weekend following Kennedy's death.

Similar Titles:
DiCamillo, Kate, ***Because of Winn Dixie.*** Candlewick, 2000, 182pp. $15.99. ISBN: 0763607762. Candlewick, 2001, 182pp. $5.99. ISBN: 0763616052. Random House Audio, 2001. $18.00. ISBN: 0807261866. Random House Audio, 2004. $19.99. CD. ISBN: 1400091497.
Holt, Kimberly Willis, ***When Zachary Beaver Came to Town.*** Holt, 1999, 240pp. $16.95. ISBN: 0805061169. Yearling, 2001, 240pp. $5.99. ISBN: 0440229049. Random House Audio, 2004. $36.00. ISBN: 0807283940.
Konigsburg, E.L., ***A View from Saturday.*** Atheneum, 1996, 163pp. $16.95. ISBN: 068980993X. Aladdin, 1998, 176pp. $5.99. ISBN: 0689817215. Random House Audio, 2001. $25.00. ISBN: 0807204692. Random House Audio, 2004, $35.00. CD. ISBN: 1400089921.
Martin, Ann M., ***Belle Teale.*** Scholastic, 2001, 214pp. $15.95. ISBN: 0439098238. Scholastic, 2004, 224pp. $4.99. ISBN: 0439098246.
Spinelli, Jerry, ***Maniac Magee.*** Little Brown, 1990, 184pp. $15.95. ISBN: 0316807222. Little Brown, 1999, 180pp. $6.99. ISBN: 0316809063. Random House Audio, 2001. $25.00. ISBN: 0807205958. Random House Audio, 2005. $19.95. CD. ISBN: 0307243184.

53 Mead, Alice, *Year of No Rain.*

Farrar, Straus & Giroux, 2003, 130pp. $16.00. ISBN: 0374372888. Random House, 2005, 144pp. $5.50. ISBN: 0440420040.

Web Site: <http://home.maine.rr.com/aliceme>
Subjects: Africans, Brothers and Sisters, Kidnapping, Refugees, Survival, Violence, War
Genres: International, Multicultural
Levels: BL 5-7, K 3-7, PW 3-7, SLJ 5-7

Annotation: After soldiers have attacked his village, 11-year-old Stephen returns from hiding to find his mother dead and his sister gone. With little food or water, Stephen and his two friends set out across the Sudan to find a refugee camp where they can get help. Stephen uses his geography book to determine where they are.

Booktalk: Stephen's life was boring. Every morning he and his friend Wol took the village cows out to graze. Sometimes they practiced throwing their spears at gourds, but mostly they just lay on the ground in what little shade they could find and talked. Wol was only 14 but he wanted to marry Stephen's sister Naomi. He told Stephen that he would give his family five cows, the same number of cows the old man in the village offered for Naomi. Since Naomi did not want to marry an old man, Wol's and Naomi's engagement was formalized that night in front of the whole village. Their happiness came to an abrupt halt however, when rebel troops raided the village, killing and looting. Fearing they would be kidnapped and forced into service, Stephen and Wol hid in the tall grass until the soldiers were gone. But, when they returned to the burned out village they could not find Naomi alive or amongst the bodies. Had the soldiers taken Wol's bride-to-be with them?

Excerpt: Page 3 through first two lines on page 5.

Curriculum Connections: Math, Social Studies
When the boys set out into the desert to find a refugee camp Stephen uses his geography book to determine how far they must walk. Have students use library media center resources to locate maps of the Sudan and determine a route from a location in the Sudan to the largest body of water, computing the miles as well as how many days it would take to walk this distance.

Similar Titles:

Farmer, Nancy, ***The Eye, the Ear, and the Arm.*** Orchard, 1994, 320pp. $18.95. ISBN: 0531068293. Penguin Putnam, 1995, 311pp. $5.99. ISBN: 0140376410.
Farmer, Nancy, ***A Girl Named Disaster.*** Orchard, 1996, 309pp. $19.95. ISBN: 0531095398. Penguin Putman, 1998, 306pp. $5.99. ISBN: 0140386351.
McKissack, Patricia C., ***Nzingha: Warrior Queen of Matamba, Angola, Africa, 1595.*** The Royal Diaries Series. Scholastic, 2000, 144pp. $10.95. ISBN: 0439112109.
McKissack, Patricia C., ***The Royal Kingdoms of Ghana, Mali and Songhay: Life in Medieval Africa.*** Holt, 1995, 142pp. $9.95. ISBN: 0805042598.
Naidoo, Beverley, ***Journey to Jo'burg: A South African Story.*** HarperCollins, 1999, 96pp. $16.89. ISBN: 0397321694. HarperCollins, 1998, 96pp. $4.99. ISBN: 0064402371.

54 Myers, Anna, *Stolen by the Sea.*
Walker, 2001. 160pp. $16.95. ISBN: 0802787878.

Subjects: Fathers and Daughters, Mexican Americans, Natural Disasters, Orphans, Self-Esteem, Survival
Genres: Adventure, Historical, Multicultural
Levels: K 5-8, SLJ 5-8

Annotation: Twelve-year-old Maggie, a spoiled rich girl, and Felipe, a 14-year-old Mexican orphan, must work together to survive the Galveston, Texas hurricane of 1900 as the wall of water destroys the house around them.

Booktalk: I know he wishes I were a boy. I wish I was born a boy. Then maybe Father would pay as much attention to me as he does to that Filipe. As far as I am concerned Filipe shouldn't even be allowed in the house – he's an orphan from Mexico. What does Father think he is doing acting like this ragged boy is his long lost son? It is so unfair that he teaches that boy things he would never teach me. It's not fair that girls are treated differently than boys. And now with Mother about to have a baby, it is even worse. Father is ignoring me even more than he usually does. What if this baby is a boy? If it is I may as well not even be here! Who cares that they are going to the doctor's in Houston and aren't taking me? Who cares that the housekeeper says that there is a storm coming and that maybe they won't get back to Galveston tonight. I don't care – I am not going to spend time with that Filipe no matter what, even if the storm comes right through the middle of my bedroom.

Excerpt: Page 87, third paragraph to end of fifth paragraph on page 89.

Curriculum Connection: Social Studies
The Hurricane of 1900 destroyed a good portion of Galveston. Have students use library media center resources to learn about the storm and how the residents dealt with the storm's destruction.

Similar Titles:
Challoner, Jack, ***Hurricane and Tornado.*** Eyewitness Books. DK Publishing, 2004, 72pp. $19.99. ISBN: 0756606896.
Garland, Sherry, ***Silent Storm.*** Harcourt, 1993, 288pp. $14.95. ISBN: 0152741704. Harcourt, 1995, 288pp. $6.00. ISBN: 015200016X.
Jones, Martha Tannery, ***Terror from the Gulf: A Hurricane in Galveston.*** Hendrick-Long, 1995, 134pp. $17.95. ISBN: 1885777213.
Nicolson, Cynthia Pratt, ***Hurricane!*** The Disaster Series. Kids Can Press, 2002, 32pp. $14.95. ISBN: 1550749064. Kids Can Press, 2002, 32pp. $6.95. ISBN: 1550749706.
Rogers, Lisa Waller, ***Great Storm: The Hurricane Diary of T.J. King, Galveston, Texas, 1900.*** Texas Tech, 2002, 192pp. $14.50. ISBN: 0896724786.

Myers, Walter Dean, *A Time to Love: Stories from the Old Testament.*

Scholastic, 2003, 127pp. $19.95. ISBN: 0439220009.

Subjects: Family Problems, Relationships, Religion
Genre: Multicultural, Short Stories
Levels: BL 7-10, PW 7 up, SLJ 7 up

Annotation: Often told from a secondary character's point of view, first person retellings of six stories from the Old Testament explore the depth of human love, faith, and betrayal.

Booktalk: Would you do something someone you care about asked you to even if you knew you could get hurt? What if he or she told you to walk down a dark alley at night, with a bunch of thugs waiting at the other end to beat you up, to prove you cared about them? Would you do it? Sounds pretty dumb, right? Well, through the ages, men and women have done some pretty self-destructive things to prove their love. Let's take, for example, one of the characters in this collection of short stories. His name is Samson. Remember him? Samson was a very physically strong man, but he had an emotional weakness and her name was Delilah. Delilah knew about the one physical weakness Samson had and she used it to destroy him. There are five other stories in this collection, about Bible characters you may know, but they are all told with a bit of twist.

Excerpt: Page 34, first paragraph, through last paragraph on page 35.

Curriculum Connection: Art
Christopher Myers uses a variety of artistic styles to create the accompanying illustrations. Have students use library media center resources to locate examples of art that are rendered in the variety of styles used for this collection's illustrations. Based on what they learned about the different art techniques, have students choose one of the styles and create an illustration for a story in the collection.

Similar Titles:
Goldin, Barbara Diamond, ***Journeys with Elijah: Eight Tales of the Prophet.*** Harcourt, 1999, 96pp. $20.00. ISBN: 0152004459.
Hunter, Elrose, ***The Story Atlas of the Bible.*** Silver Burdett, 1995. 64pp. $15.95. ISBN: 0382391020. Silver Burdett, 1995, 64pp. $8.95. ISBN: 0382391039.
Manushkin, Fran, ***Daughters of Fire: Heroines of the Bible.*** Harcourt, 2001, 88pp. $20.00. ISBN: 0152018697.
Paulsen, Gary, ***The Tent: A Parable in One Sitting.*** Bantam Doubleday Dell, 1996, 86pp. $4.99. ISBN: 0440219191.
Yolen, Jane and Bruce Coville, ***Armageddon Summer.*** Harcourt, 1998, 272pp. $17.00. ISBN: 0152017674. Harcourt, 1999, 266pp. $5.99. ISBN: 0152022686.

56 Naidoo, Beverley, *The Other Side of Truth.*

HarperCollins, 2001, 272pp. $17.89. ISBN: 0060296291. HarperTrophy, 2003, 252pp. $5.99. ISBN: 0064410021.

Web Site: <www.beverleynaidoo.com>
Subjects: Africans, Brothers and Sisters, Crime, Death, Grieving, Murder, Refugees, Violence
Genres: International, Multicultural, Realistic
Lists: 2002 BBYA, 2002 CN, 2002 TC
Levels: BL 6-10, K 5-9, PW 5 up, SLJ 5-8

Annotation: When their mother is killed, their journalist father, who is in trouble with the government, pays to have 12-year-old Sade and her younger brother smuggled out of Nigeria by a woman who then abandons them on the streets of London. Sade turns to a newscaster for help.

Booktalk: Sade was numb with grief when she walked out of the room where her father sat with her dead mother in his arms. Her mother was covered in blood, her own blood. The doctor said there was no chance for her – the shot was straight through the heart. Sade felt the pain of her mother's death in her own heart. She was numb with pain and wasn't thinking about what she was doing when the phone rang. Of course she picked it up. It didn't matter to Sade who was calling. She just picked it up and automatically said hello. At the other end the caller didn't care who answered it – just so it was answered while they were all still in shock. He had a clear and deadly message for Sade's father – "if we get the family first, what does it matter?" It was time to get Sade and her younger brother Femi out of Nigeria, but they did not have passports. So it was arranged for the siblings to travel to London as the children of Mrs. Bankole, a loud and flashy woman who wore too many rings and dressed in ridiculous clothes, ones Sade knew her own mother would never wear. Sade sat next to Mrs. Bankole pretending to be her daughter and wishing this trip to London, and why she and Femi were forced to take it, was all a very bad nightmare. She closed her eyes and wished she were asleep and that her mother would be there when she awoke, telling her it was just a bad dream. But, that isn't going to happen. Sade is going to have to dig deep inside to find the strength to survive what happens next in London.

Excerpt: (pbk.) Page 3 to break on page 6.

Curriculum Connection: Social Studies
Have students use library media center resources to research Nigeria and the political situation that forces some people to flee the country by any means possible. Have them discuss why the Nigerians would want to come to the United States.

Similar Titles:

Ellis, Deborah, ***The Breadwinner.*** Groundwood Books, 2001, 172pp. $15.99. ISBN: 0888994192. Groundwood Books, 2001, 170pp. $5.95. ISBN: 0888994168. Random House Audio, 2002. $18.00. ISBN: 0807209732.

Hussein, Ikram, ***Teenage Refugees from Somalia Speak Out.*** In Their Own Voices Series. Rosen, 1997, 64pp. $16.95. ISBN: 0823924440.

Murphy, Patricia J., ***Nigeria.*** Marshall Cavendish, 2004, 48pp. $17.95. ISBN: 0761417958.

Naidoo, Beverley, ***Chain of Fire.*** HarperCollins, 1993, 242pp. $5.99. ISBN: 0064404684.

Naidoo, Beverley, ***No Turning Back: A Novel of South Africa.*** HarperTrophy, 1999, 208pp. $5.99. ISBN: 0064407497.

Nelson, Theresa, *Ruby Electric.*

57

Atheneum, 2003, 272pp. $16.95. ISBN: 068985384X. Simon & Schuster, 2004, 272pp. $5.99. ISBN: 0689871465.

Web Site: <www.theresanelson.net>
Subjects: Artists, Brothers and Sisters, Divorce, Family Problems, Friendship, Moving, Schools, Writing
Genres: Realistic
Lists: 2004 CN
Levels: BL 5-8, K 5-7, PW 5-7, SLJ 5-8

Annotation: Twelve-year-old Ruby writes screenplays to deal with her father's five-year absence and their move from Texas to Los Angeles. With the help of two misfits in her class, Ruby and her little brother Pete paint a prehistoric mural on the concrete sides of the Los Angeles River, bringing the residents of their neighborhood together.

Booktalk: We sat in the booth for what seemed like hours and he didn't show up – again. I tried to eat as slow as possible in case he was running late, but Mom had enough of my stalling. She paid the bill and we walked out of the café. I hadn't seen my father in over five years and Petey, my little brother, didn't even know him. Petey was only a baby when he left. No matter how many times, and in how many different ways, I asked Mom why my father had to go away she wouldn't tell me. My mom was what you call a "closed book" when it came to my father. Well, one of these days I am going to find him and ask him right to his face why he left us. I am going to open that book up wide, whether she likes it or not. But until then I am going to write my own scenes of how we will meet again, my father and me. For now I'll write my own versions of our meeting, in a book that I can open wide and read, and even change, any time I want to.

Excerpt: Page 23.

Curriculum Connections: Art, Language Arts

Ruby writes her own screenplays. Using library media center collections of plays as examples, discuss how plays are written and the various elements included. Divide students up into small groups to write a short screenplay based on one of the events in the book. Collaborate with the art teacher to help the students design the stage scenery and costumes to present their one-act plays.

Similar Titles:

Avi, ***Blue Heron.*** Morrow, 1993, 192pp. $5.99. ISBN: 0380720434. Recorded Books, 1994. $27.00. ISBN: 0788700081.

Bauer, Joan, ***Stand Tall.*** Penguin Putnam, 2002, 192pp. $16.99. ISBN: 039923473X. Penguin, 2004, 192pp. $6.99. ISBN: 014240148X.

Blume, Judy, ***It's Not the End of the World.*** Atheneum, 2002, 176pp. $17.00. ISBN: 0689842937. Yearling, 1986, 176pp. $5.50. ISBN: 0440441587.

Brooks, Bruce, ***What Hearts.*** HarperCollins, 1992, 208pp. $16.95. ISBN: 0060211318. HarperCollins, 1999, 208pp. $5.99. ISBN: 0064471276.

Danziger, Paula, ***The Divorce Express.*** Penguin, 1998, 160pp. $5.99. ISBN: 0698116852.

58 Paver, Michelle, *Wolf Brother.*

The Chronicles of Ancient Darkness. HarperCollins, 2005, 304pp. $17.89. ISBN: 0060728264. HarperCollinsAudio, 2005. $27.95. CD. ISBN: 0060758384.

Web Site: <www.michellepaver.com>
Subjects: Animals, Death, Fathers and Sons, Folklore, Friendship, Grieving, Journeys, Magic, Prehistoric Man, Survival, Violence, Wolves
Genres: Fantasy, Supernatural
Levels: PW 5 up, SLJ 5-9

Annotation: After his father's death, 12-year-old Torak is left alone to fight an enormous bear that is killing every living thing in its path. With the help of Renn, a girl of the Forest Clan, and guided by Wolf, an orphan wolf pup, Torak must journey to the Mountain of the World Spirit and ask the Spirit to vanquish the demon possessed bear.

Booktalk: Death exploded out of the forest so fast that Torak and his father did not have time to protect themselves. The demon bear threw Torak against a tree, tore open Torak's father's side, and melted back into the forest as silent as a mist. Torak knew normal bears did not stalk men, but this was no normal bear. His father said the bear was possessed by a demon and Torak was the only one who could destroy it. As he lay bleeding to death, Torak's father made Torak promise that he would find the Mountain of the Death Spirit. His father then urged Torak to prepare him quickly for his Death Journey. Torak was at the river, getting his father a last drink of water, when the bear returned. His father screamed, "Torak, run!" and Torak did. He ran away from his father's dying screams. He ran until he could run no more, but Torak's running is far from over. The demon bear is after him now. Will Torak make it to the Mountain of the Death Spirit or meet death on the way?

Excerpt: Page 5, starting with "In the forest..." to third to last paragraph on page 8.

Curriculum Connection: Science

Have the students read the Author's Note at the end of the book and choose a topic of interest to research using library media center resources, such as early tools, clothing, extinct animals, or the Clan structure of early man. Have them share what they have learned through a recreated artifact from the time, a drawing, or an oral report.

Similar Titles:

Corder, Zizou, ***Lionboy.*** Dial, 2003, 288pp. $15.99. ISBN: 0803729820. Penguin, 2004, 275pp. $6.99. ISBN: 0142402265. Highbridge Audio, 2003. $29.95. ISBN: 1565118308. Highbridge Audio, 2003. $29.95. CD. ISBN: 1565118316.

George, Jean Craighead, ***Julie.*** HarperCollins, 1996, 227pp. $5.99. ISBN: 0064405737.

Hoshikawa, Jun, ***Beringia: Bridge of Spirits.*** Viz Communications, 1999, 200pp. $16.95. ISBN: 1569312966.

Jones, Diana Wynne, ***The Spellcoats.*** The Dalemark Quartet. Greenwillow, 2001, 288pp. $16.95. ISBN: 0060298731. HarperCollins, 2001, 304pp. $6.99. ISBN: 0064473155.

Pierce, Tamora, ***Wolf-Speaker.*** The Immortals Series. Simon & Schuster, 2003, 204pp. $10.95. ISBN: 0689856121. Random House 1997, 304pp. $5.99. ISBN: 0679882898.

Pierce, Tamora, *Alanna: The First Adventure.*

59

The Song of the Lioness Quartet. Atheneum, 2002, 216pp. $11.95. ISBN: 0689853238. Knopf, 1997. 240pp. $5.50. ISBN: 0679801146. Random House Audio, 2000. $22.00. ISBN: 0807261726.

Web Site: <www.tamora-pierce.com>
Subjects: Brothers and Sisters, Knights and Knighthood, Magic, Occupations, Self-Identity, Sexuality
Genres: Adventure, Fantasy
Levels: PW 5 up, SLJ 5-8

Annotation: Eleven-year-old Alanna and her twin brother Thom switch identities when they are sent off to the convent and to the castle. Alanna, disguised as the young page, Alan, trains to be a knight while Thom trains to become a sorcerer.

Booktalk: Yes, I really am a girl, but I keep my hair short and I never undress in front of the other pages. No matter how hot it gets outside, even when I'm sweaty and miserable, I don't jump into the swimming hole with them. How did I get away with switching places with my brother? It was easy. Father doesn't pay any attention to what my twin brother Thom and I do. No one even noticed when I rode off to the castle while Thom road off to the convent. Why shouldn't I become a knight? I have always been better with a sword than Thom. He never wanted to be a knight. He wants to be a great sorcerer. Me – I don't want anything to do with the magic I know I have inside of me. I want it to go away so I can concentrate on my training. One day I will be a great knight, you just wait and see.

Excerpt: Page 45, from the new section, to the second to last paragraph on page 46.

Curriculum Connection: Social Studies
Alanna was expected to go to the convent and learn the skills of being a lady. Have students use library media center resources to research and compare the social mores of the Middle Ages with today. Have them discuss how society has changed in relation to what are now suitable activities for girls.

Similar Titles:

Pierce, Tamora, *In the Hand of the Goddess.* The Song of the Lioness Quartet. Atheneum, 2002, 209pp. $10.95. ISBN: 0689853246. Random House, 1997, 240pp. $5.50. ISBN: 0679801111. Random House Audio, 2001. $25.00. ISBN: 0807206040.
Pierce, Tamora, *Lady Knight.* The Protector of the Small Series. Random House, 2002, 429pp. $16.95. ISBN: 0375814655. Random House, 2003, 448pp. $5.99. ISBN: 037581471X.
Pierce, Tamora, *Lioness Rampant.* The Song of the Lioness Quartet. Atheneum, 2003, 314pp. $10.95. ISBN: 0689854307. Simon & Schuster, 2005, 400pp. $5.99. ISBN: 0689878575. Random House Audio, 2002. $26.00. ISBN: 0807206105.
Pierce, Tamora, *Page.* The Protector of the Small Series. Random House, 2000, 272pp. $16.00. ISBN: 0679889159. Random House, 2001, 288pp. $5.99. ISBN: 0679889183.
Pierce, Tamora, *The Woman Who Rides Like a Man.* The Song of the Lioness Quartet. Atheneum, 2003, 240pp. $10.95. ISBN: 0689854293. Random House, 1997, 256pp. $5.50. ISBN: 067980112X. Random House Audio, 2002. $26.00. ISBN: 0807206075.

Pratchett, Terry, *The Amazing Maurice and His Educated Rodents.*

HarperCollins, 2001, 256pp. $17.89. ISBN: 006001234X. HarperTrophy, 2003, 340pp. $6.99. ISBN: 0060012358.

Web Site: <www.terrypratchettbooks.com>
Subjects: Cats, Folklore, Magic, Music, Rats
Genres: Fantasy
Lists: 2002 BBYA
Levels: BL 6-9, PW 7 up, SLJ 7 up

Annotation: Maurice, a con artist cat with the ability to talk, leads a band of talking rats and a pipe-playing boy who convinces village after village that he can rid them of their rats. That is until they enter Bad Blintz and run into a band of Rat Catchers, a quirky Mayor's daughter, and the Rat King.

Booktalk: Have any of you heard or read the Pied Piper of Hamlin story? The one about the piper who leads the children out of Hamlin because the Mayor didn't pay him what he promised for ridding the town of rats? Well, imagine if the mastermind behind a similar rat ridding scheme is a talking cat. Matter of fact, a con artist genius of a cat named Maurice. You see, Maurice ate a rat that had eaten scraps from the wizards' trash heap. You never know what magical potions get thrown into wizards' trash heaps, including ones that can make animals, in this case a cat and a band of rats, as smart as humans. Journey with Maurice and his band of rats as they attempt to re-enact their rat-ridding scheme in the town of Bad Blintz. The name of the town, Bad Blintz, should have given them pause, but Maurice was pretty sure of himself at this point and the rats just wanted this to be their last con job. Maurice, his pied piper boy, and his rats should have kept going to the next town. Bad Blintz was not going to be like any of the other towns they had so easily conned.

Excerpt: Second to last paragraph on page 11 through page 13.

Curriculum Connections: Social Studies, Language Arts
Share various versions of the Pied Piper tale found in library media center resources and have students write their own version of the Pied Piper of Hamlin, setting it in a time period or location of their choice.

Similar Titles:
Adams, Richard, *Tales from Watership Down.* Avon, 1998, 352pp. $6.99. ISBN: 0380729342.
Adams, Richard, *Watership Down.* Simon & Schuster, 1996. 448pp. $27.50. ISBN: 068483605X. Avon, 1976, 496pp. $7.99. ISBN: 0380002930.
Browning, Robert, *The Pied Piper of Hamlin.* Knopf, 1993, 104pp. $12.95. ISBN 0679428127. Dover Publications, 1997, 48pp. $7.95. ISBN: 0486296199.

Jarvis, Robin, *The Alchemist's Cat.* The Deptford Histories Chronicles, 2004, 320pp. $17.95. ISBN: 1587172577.

Richardson, Bill, *After Hamelin.* Annick Press, 2000, 144pp. $19.95. ISBN: 1550376292. Annick Press, 2000, 144pp. $8.95. ISBN: 1550376284.

Pratchett, Terry, *A Hat Full of Sky: The Continuing Adventures of Tiffany Aching and the Wee Free Men.*

The Discworld Series. HarperCollins, 2004. $17.89. ISBN: 0060586613. HarperTrophy, 2005, 384pp. $6.99. ISBN: 0060586621. HarperChildrensAudio, 2005. $34.95. CD. ISBN: 0060747684.

Web Site: <www.terrypratchettbooks.com>
Subjects: Friendship, Magic, Witchcraft
Genres: Humor, Fantasy
Lists: 2005 BBYA, 2005 CN
Levels: BL 6-10, SLJ 5-8, V 7 up

Annotation: Tiffany is a witch-in-training with Miss Level, a witch with two bodies. Using her powers when she shouldn't, Tiffany draws a hiver, a disembodied presence that seeks out and craves power, which tries to take over her mind.

Booktalk: Don't you just hate it when someone tells you that you can't do something, especially if it is something that you are the only one you know who can do it? This is the case with Tiffany. You see, she is a witch, a young witch with powers beyond even what she can imagine. And, Tiffany is new to her powers. She doesn't quite know how to handle them properly yet. Nor does she know when *not* to use them. She's been told that if she uses them incorrectly she could hurt herself and others. But, as much as she tries not to use them when she shouldn't, she can't help but try them out once in awhile, now can she? She figures it must be okay if she practices when she is alone and no one is watching her. What she doesn't know is that there is something out there watching – a disembodied something, an evil something, just waiting for her to use her powers at the wrong time so it can take over her mind.

Curriculum Connection: Language Arts
Have students select a novel from the library media center with a magical main character. After reading their chosen novel, have them write a story about what might happen if this character and Tiffany met during a meeting of the young witches in *A Hat Full of Sky*.

Similar Titles:
Duncan, Lois, *Gallows Hill.* Bantam Doubleday Dell, 1998, 240pp. $5.50. ISBN: 440227259.

Pratchett, Terry, ***Equal Rites.*** The Discworld Series. HarperCollins, 2000, 240pp. $6.99. ISBN: 0061020699.

Pratchett, Terry, ***The Wee Free Men.*** The Discworld Series. HarperCollins, 2003, 263pp. $17.89. ISBN: 0060012374. HarperCollins, 2004, 375pp. $6.99. ISBN: 0060012382. HarperChildrensAudio, 2003. $29.95. ISBN: 0060566256. HarperChildrensAudio, 2005. $29.95. CD. ISBN: 0060785985.

Pratchett, Terry, ***Witches Abroad.*** The Discworld Series. HarperCollins, 2002, 384pp. $6.99. ISBN: 0061020613.

Pratchett, Terry, ***Wyrd Sisters.*** The Discworld Series. HarperCollins, 2001, 288pp. $6.99. ISBN: 0061020664.

Rinaldi, Ann, *Nine Days a Queen: The Short Life and Reign of Lady Jane Grey.*

62

HarperCollins, 2005, 192pp. $16.89. ISBN: 0060549246.

Web Site: <www.annrinaldi.com>
Subjects: Crime, Mothers and Daughters, Murder, Religion, Violence
Genres: Historical, International
Levels: BL 6-8, K 5-9

Annotation: Lady Jane Grey, the fifth in line for the throne of England, is summoned to court by Katharine, wife of Henry VIII, and "adopted" by Sir Thomas Seymour who is later beheaded for treason. Young King Edward VI dies and 15-year-old Jane becomes queen, but is beheaded by Mary the Queen of England.

Booktalk: I am too young for this. I should not know about the intrigue that goes on in the royal chambers. King Henry VIII scares me silly with his tempers. And now I have to go into his bedchamber and plead for the life of his wife, Lady Katharine. How Sir Wriothesley could be so despicable I do not know. He has accused Lady Katharine of treason because she is intrigued by Martin Luther's words. She once gave me a book about this new religion. I had the book in my hand when Sir Wriothesley met me in the hallway. He wanted me to spy on her. Of course, he didn't say it quite that way – he said I could serve the King well by telling him how Lady Katharine goes with this Martin Luther madness. When I pointedly asked if he meant spying, he just smiled and said I would only be protecting Lady Katharine. Well, I am protecting her – from him. I am about to walk into the King's chamber and plead for her life. This is a form of protection I would prefer *not* to be involved in, but I really have no choice. Wriothesley wants to see Lady Katharine beheaded.

Excerpt: Page 11 through end of the last paragraph on page 14.

Curriculum Connection: Social Studies

Henry VIII had several wives and a number of children. Have students use library media center materials to research Henry VIII's extended family and work in groups to create a family tree for each of his wives and their children.

Similar Titles:

Davis, Kenneth C., ***Don't Know Much About Kings and Queens of England.*** HarperCollins, 2002, 48pp. $15.89. ISBN: 0060286121.

Greenblatt, Miriam, ***Elizabeth I and Tudor England.*** The Rulers and Their Times Series. Marshall Cavendish, 2001, 80pp. $19.95. ISBN: 0761410287.

Lasky, Kathryn, ***Elizabeth I: Red Rose of the House of Tudor, England, 1544.*** The Royal Diaries Series. Scholastic, 1999, 237pp. $10.95. ISBN: 0590684841.

Meyer, Caroline, ***Mary, Bloody Mary.*** The Young Royals Series. Harcourt, 1999, 227pp. $17.00. ISBN: 0152019065. Harcourt, 2001, 240pp. $6.00. ISBN: 0152164561.

Meyer, Caroline, ***Patience, Princess Catherine.*** The Young Royals Series. Harcourt, 2004, 208pp. $17.00. ISBN: 0152165444. Harcourt 2005, 208pp. $5.95. ISBN: 0152054472.

63 Roberts, Willo Davis, *Rebel.*

Atheneum, 2003. $15.95. ISBN: 0689850735. Simon & Schuster, 2005, 160pp. $4.99. ISBN: 0689850816.

Web Site: <www.willodavisroberts.com>
Subjects: Crime, Dogs, Elderly, Friendship, Grandmothers
Genres: Mystery, Realistic
Levels: BL 4-6, K 5-8, SLJ 6-8

Annotation: Amanda, called Rebel because of her willful nature, and laid back Moses spend the summer helping their grandmothers clean up an old boarding house and, with the help of a very protective dog, solve a mysterious robbery and stop a counterfeit money scheme.

Booktalk: Do you ever feel like you just don't belong in your family? Well, that is certainly the case with me. My nickname is Rebel for good reason. My first word was "NO!" and some of my scars are from just plain stubbornness. I know that – but that's just the way it is. Like how I got my broken arm when I was a kid. It didn't matter that I was in the tree and Wally was on the ground – it was *my* bear. I know I could have just let go when I started falling out of the tree, but that was not the point. It was *my* bear. And it wasn't like I was really lost that time Mom panicked – I knew right where I was – in the herpetology exhibit at the zoo. Staying the night at the zoo sounded like fun so I just didn't get back on the bus with the other kids. And studying those snakes for hours without anyone bothering me was really cool. So what's Mom's problem with me spending the summer with Gram? It isn't like I can't take care of myself. What trouble can I get into while helping Gram fix up the old house she bought to rent out rooms to college students?

Excerpt: Page 11 through third paragraph on page 15.

Curriculum Connections: Science, Social Studies
Rebel and Moses get involved in solving a counterfeit money scam. Have students use library media center resources to research the changes in the process for printing money to ensure that counterfeit money is not easily mistaken for the real thing.

Similar Titles:
Kehret, Peg, **Danger at the Fair.** Penguin, 2002, 144pp. $5.99. ISBN: 0142302228.
Nixon, Joan Lowery, **Shadowmaker.** Dell, 1995, 208pp. $4.99. ISBN: 0440219426. Recorded Books, 2001. $36.00. ISBN: 0788751859.
Roberts, Willo Davis, **Buddy is a Stupid Name for a Girl.** Atheneum, 2001, 224pp. $16.00. ISBN: 0689816707. Simon & Schuster, 2002, 224pp. $4.99. ISBN: 0689851642.
Roberts, Willo Davis, **Twisted Summer.** Simon & Schuster, 1998, 192pp. $4.99. ISBN: 0689806000.
Van Draanen, Wendelin, **Sammy Keyes and the Sisters of Mercy.** The Sammy Keyes Series. Random House, 1999, 210pp. $15.95. ISBN: 0679888527. Random House, 1999, 224pp. $5.99. ISBN: 0375801839. Live Oak Media, 2001. $29.95. ISBN: 0874997275.

Sage, Angie, *Magyk.*

The Septimus Heap Series. HarperCollins, 2005, 576pp. $17.89. ISBN: 0060577320. HarperCollinsAudio, 2005. $27.95. CD. ISBN: 0060760834.

Web Site: <www.septimusheap.com> (book site, not author site)
Subjects: Infants, Kidnapping, Magic, Orphans, Self-Identity, Wizards
Genres: Fantasy
Levels: PW 4 up

Annotation: Silas Heap finds a baby girl left in the forest the same night that the midwife proclaims his infant son Septimus dead. When Jenni is 10 years old the Heaps learn that she is a princess and the heir to the throne. The Heaps go into hiding with Aunt Zelda, the Keeper of Marram Marshes, taking along Boy 412 from the Young Army, who just got in the way during their escape, but who turns out to be the wizard Septimus Heap, the seventh son of the seventh son.

Booktalk: I'm Boy 412, from the Young Army. They take us away from our families when we are babies and give us a number rather than a name so I don't know who my parents are. I have lived in the barracks with the other boys all of my life and we did what we were told no matter how miserable the duty was. My last duty was standing guard outside the Wizard Tower. It was so cold outside I was freezing in the thin clothes they give us. But even if I died of the cold, that is the role of a Boy in the Young Army – do what you are told and ask no questions. I wasn't about to complain. I know what happens when a Boy does that. Anyway, the last thing I remember was shaking so hard from the cold that my teeth hurt. Then I woke up in the ExtraOrdinary Wizard's rooms, wearing a pair of nice warm pajamas. Before I could say, "I can't be in here!" the door flew open and the Assassin came in and shouted, "You're under arrest!" I knew she was talking to me so I got up and walked toward her, but she pushed me out of the way and grabbed for the girl in the room. The next thing I knew there was a loud CRACK and someone grabbed me and threw me down the rubbish chute. The rubbish chute – I hate confined places and I am going to be in so much trouble when I get out of this mess that I have no idea how I got myself into in the first place. And I don't think I am going to be going back to my regular life even if I do fall out of the other end of this chute. Not when the Assassin is involved.

Excerpt: Page 26 through page 29.

Curriculum Connection: Social Studies

Have students use library media center materials to research Hitler's Youth and compare the role of the Young Army boys in *Magyk* to the role that German school-age boys played during WWII.

Similar Titles:

Barron, T.A., ***The Lost Years of Merlin.*** Philomel, 1996, 326pp. $19.99. ISBN: 0399230181. Penguin, 1999, 284pp. $6.99. ISBN: 044100668X. Random House Audio, 2000. $30.00. ISBN: 080726170X.

Colfer, Eoin, ***Artemis Fowl.*** The Artemis Fowl Series. Miramax, 2001, 277pp. $16.95. ISBN: 0786808012. Hyperion, 2003, 316pp. $5.99. ISBN: 0786817879. Random House Audio, 2004. $26.00. ISBN: 0807208892. Random House Audio, 2004. $28.00. CD. ISBN: 1400085861.

Duane, Diane, ***A Wizard Alone.*** The Young Wizards Series. Harcourt, 2002, 336pp. $17.00. ISBN: 0152045627. Harcourt, 2003, 352pp. $6.95. ISBN: 0152049118.

Koller, Jackie French, ***The Wizard's Apprentice.*** The Keepers Series. Aladdin, 2003, 192pp. $4.99. ISBN: 0689855923.

Rowling, J.K., ***Harry Potter and the Sorcerer's Stone.*** Scholastic, 1998, 309pp. $19.95. ISBN: 0590353403. Scholastic, 1999, 312pp. $6.99. ISBN: 059035342X. Random House Audio, 1999. $35.00. ISBN: 0807281751. Random House Audio, 1999. $49.95. CD. ISBN: 0807281956.

Skurzynski, Gloria, *Virtual War.*
The Virtual Wars Chronologs. Simon & Schuster, 1997, 152pp. $16.00. ISBN: 0689813740. Simon & Schuster, 2004, 192pp. $5.99. ISBN: 0689867859.

Web Site: <http://gloriabooks.com>
Subjects: Disabilities, Medical Experimentation, Self-Identity, War
Genres: Science Fiction
Lists: 1998 BBYA, 1998 QP
Levels: BL 6-9, K 5-9, PW 5-9, SLJ 5-8, V 6-9

Annotation: Fourteen-year-old, genetically engineered Corgan fights a virtual war for one of the few pieces of inhabitable land left on Earth, with a 14-year-old female code breaker and a 10-year-old mutant strategist.

Booktalk: How many of you like to play strategy games on the computer or in the arcades? Are there times you get so into the game that you feel like there isn't another human being in the world? To Corgan, there really hasn't been another human being in his world. For the last 14 years, his entire life, he has lived in a box and has had interaction with a virtual nurturer, but that's it. Corgan was genetically created and he doesn't have a family. He has never seen another human, let alone another teenager. So you can imagine how confused he is when the first human he meets not only turns out to be another teenager, but a girl. Now how is he supposed to keep his mind on fighting a virtual war after seeing her? It gets even harder for Corgan to concentrate and not kill those little soldiers on his screen when he learns that this blonde girl is to be his code-breaker and the little mutant kid with her is to be his strategist. A girl and a mutant kid? How is he not supposed to stare at them?

Excerpt: First paragraph on page 18 through page 22.

Curriculum Connection: Social Studies
In this book Earth's inhabitants live in domed cities because of nuclear contaminants. Have students use library media center resources to determine if there is a location on earth that has been so contaminated by nuclear waste that humans cannot live there and the potential of human habitation in the future.

Similar Titles:
Armstrong, Jennifer, ***The Kindling.*** The Fire-Us Trilogy. HarperCollins, 2002, 224pp. $15.89. ISBN: 0060294116. Morrow, 2003, 304pp. $5.99. ISBN: 0064472736. Horowitz, Anthony, ***Point Blank.*** The Alex Rider Adventure Series. Philomel, 2002, 215pp. $17.99. ISBN: 039923621X. Penguin, 2004, 304pp. $5.99. ISBN: 0142401641. Skurzynski, Gloria, ***Clones.*** The Virtual War Chronologs. Atheneum, 2002, 163pp. $16.00. ISBN: 0689842635. Simon & Schuster, 2004, 208pp. $5.99. ISBN: 0689842643. Sleator, William, ***Interstellar Pig.*** Penguin, 1995, 197pp. $6.99. ISBN: 0140375953. Taylor, Theodore, ***The Bomb.*** HarperCollins, 1997, 160pp. $5.99. ISBN: 0380727234.

66 Sleator, William, *Oddballs.*
Penguin, 1995, 134pp. $5.99. ISBN: 0140374388.

Subjects: Brothers and Sisters, Friendship
Genres: Humor, Short Stories
Lists: 1994 BBYA
Levels: K 6-9

Annotation: In these 10 short stories based on his early years, Sleator shares sibling pranks, eccentric parent activities, and humorous incidents in their lives.

Booktalk: Have you ever thought about what your favorite author's early years were like? When I read William Sleator's science fiction titles such as *Interstellar Pig* and *The Boxes,* I imagined a quiet, studious man who must have spent his childhood doing science experiments and quietly reading in his room. I was as far from the truth as you can get with my ideas of what Sleator was like as a kid. He grew up in an uproarious household with eccentric and quite indulgent parents. They didn't pay much attention to their children's antics. Wouldn't your parents get upset if one of your siblings was hypnotized and made to drink out of the toilet? What would your mother say if she heard you and your sister talking about what it would be like to be a BM? Can you just imagine her horror to hear you talk about the travels of a cupcake in Queen Elizabeth's digestive system? Prepare yourself to snort laugh over these "slightly" fictionalized tales of Sleator's early years.

Excerpt: Page 3 through the first paragraph on page 5.

Curriculum Connection: Language Arts
Sleator has taken episodes from his own life and embellished them to entertain the reader. Have students use library media center resources to research the childhood of one of their favorite authors and share with the other students a humorous incident from their chosen author's childhood.

Similar Titles:
Dahl, Roald, ***The Wonderful Story of Henry Sugar and Six More.*** Knopf, 2001, 240pp. $15.95. ISBN: 037581423X. Penguin, 2000, 225pp. $6.95. ISBN: 0141304707.
Elish, Dan, ***Born Too Short: The Confessions of an Eighth-Grade Basket Case.*** Atheneum, 2002, 160pp. $16.00. ISBN: 0689843860. Simon & Schuster, 2003, 160pp. $4.99. ISBN: 068986213X.
Griffiths, Andy, ***The Day My Butt Went Psycho.*** Scholastic, 2003, 240pp. $4.99. ISBN: 0439424690.
Paulsen, Gary, ***Harris and Me: A Summer Remembered.*** Harcourt, 1993, 157pp. $16.00. ISBN: 0152928774. Bantam, 1995, 160pp. $5.99. ISBN: 0440409942.
Shusterman, Neal, ***Mindbenders: Stories to Warp Your Brain.*** The Mindquakes Series. Tor, 2000, 118pp. $3.99. ISBN: 0812538722.

Spinelli, Jerry, *Loser*.

HarperCollins, 2002, 218pp. $16.89. ISBN: 0060004835. HarperTrophy, 2003, 224pp. $5.99. ISBN: 0060540745. HarperAudio, 2002. $24.00. ISBN: 0060087943.

Web Site: <www.jerryspinelli.com>
Subjects: Bullies, Fathers and Sons, Schools, Self-Esteem
Genres: Realistic
Levels: BL 3-6, K 4-6, PW 4-7, SLJ 4-6, V 6-12

Annotation: Donald Zinkoff's life is chronicled from first through sixth grade as he changes from a happy geeky little kid everyone likes to a fourth grade loser, to a sixth grade hero who almost freezes to death in a snowstorm while trying to find a lost little girl.

Booktalk: Do any of you have a nickname that you can't stand? I see some of you nodding your heads and grimacing. Maybe it is a silly or cute nickname your parents gave you when you were little. Zinkoff isn't that lucky. The kid in this book has a nickname his classmates gave him and it isn't one any of you would like to have. The problem is – Donald Zinkoff is the kind of kid who just brings it on himself. He doesn't know it, but man, sometimes he is such a loser. (Hold up the book horizontally so that the title, *Loser*, boldly written on the spine, is clearly observable. Then show the front cover and back cover, saying "Loser" with each movement of the book so the students can clearly see the title written on both the front and back covers of the book.) But, don't feel too sorry for Zinkoff, he may just prove his classmates wrong. His nickname, Loser, soon will be replaced by a nickname we would all love to have. Zinkoff is about to prove them all wrong.

Excerpt: First chapter.

Curriculum Connection: Language Arts
Highlighting the other Spinelli novels in the library media center, have students choose a Spinelli novel you will read aloud in class. After reading and discussing the novel, have students write about how they think the characters in the other Spinelli book would react to Zinkoff as a fourth grade and sixth grade classmate.

Similar Titles:
Clements, Andrew, ***Frindle***. Simon & Schuster, 1996, 105pp. $15.95. ISBN: 0689806698. Simon & Schuster, 1997, 112pp. $4.99. ISBN: 0689818769. Random House Audio, 2000. $18.00. ISBN: 0807282766. Random House Audio, 2004. $19.99. CD. ISBN: 1400095050.
Clements, Andrew, ***The Last Holiday Concert***. Simon & Schuster, 2004, 166pp. $15.95. ISBN: 0689845162. Random House Audio, 2004. $18.00. ISBN: 1400094690.

Robinson, Barbara, ***The Best School Year Ever.*** HarperCollins, 1994, 128pp. $15.89. ISBN: 0060230436. HarperCollins, 1997, 117pp. $4.99. ISBN: 0064404927. HarperCollins, 2003. $18.00. ISBN: 0060542748.

Rockwell, Thomas, ***How to Eat Fried Worms.*** Bantam Doubleday Dell, 1975, 128pp. $4.99. ISBN: 0440445450. Random House Audio, 1998. $18.00. ISBN: 0553479571.

Sachar, Louis, ***The Boy Who Lost His Face.*** Knopf, 1997, 208pp. $5.99. ISBN: 0679886222.

68. Tashjian, Janet, *Multiple Choice.*

Holt, 1999, 186pp. $16.95. ISBN: 0805060863. Scholastic, 2001, 192pp. $4.99. ISBN: 0439174848.

Web Site: <www.janettashjian.com>
Subjects: Disabilities, Emotional Problems, Schools, Self-Esteem
Genres: Realistic
Levels: BL 5-9, K 6-8, PW 5-9, SLJ 6-9

Annotation: Fourteen-year-old Monica, perfectionist and word game expert, creates a roulette type game to bring more spontaneity to her life, but playing the game results in a child being injured and Monica's obsessive disorder being brought to light.

Booktalk: I've always been this way. I count everything, several times. And, I am really good at word games. Anagrams are my favorite. That's how the idea came to me about the game I created called Multiple Choice. You see, I am not very good at just letting life happen. Spontaneity isn't something I am good at. So, this game is supposed to bring spontaneity into my life. You see I have four Scrabble titles, A through D. I just reach my hand into the bag each morning and pull a tile out and I do it. A is a normal choice, B is just plain dumb, C is mean, not like me at all, and D is charitable. It wasn't so bad when I pulled out a B. I felt dumb, really dumb, wearing my pajamas to school but I made it through the day. Then I pulled a C and that's when it all changed. I know it was mean to lock Justin in his room, but I made it like we were playing a game. How was I to know he was going to try to climb out the window? I hear it over and over again – his scream as he fell from the window and into the bushes below. And, I see it over and over again in my mind – the sight of him holding his eyes. Now I have to own up to what I have been doing. I don't have a multiple choice on this one – this is no longer a game.

Excerpt: Pages 53 and 55 through 60.

Curriculum Connection: Health
Monica suffers from an obsessive-compulsive disorder that causes her to strive for perfectionism. Have students use library media center resources to research

perfectionism type disorders similar to Monica's and brainstorm ways to help a person deal with these disorders.

Similar Titles:
Goldberg, Jan, ***Perfectionism: What's Bad About Being Too Good?*** Free Spirit, 1999. 129pp. $12.95. ISBN: 1575420627.

Harrar, George, ***Not as Crazy as I Seem.*** Houghton Mifflin, 2003, 224pp. $15.00. ISBN: 0618263659. Houghton Mifflin, 2004, 256pp. $6.99. ISBN: 0618494804.

Hesser, Terry Spencer, ***Kissing Doorknobs.*** Bantam, 1999, 160pp. $5.50. ISBN: 0440413141.

Hyman, Bruce M., ***Obsessive Compulsive Disorder.*** Twenty-First Century Books, 2003, 96pp. $26.90. ISBN: 0761327584.

Konigsburg, E.L., ***Silent to the Bone.*** Atheneum, 2000, 272pp. $16.00. ISBN: 0689836015. Aladdin, 2002, 272pp. $5.99. ISBN: 0689836023. Random House Audio, 2000. $25.00. ISBN: 0807261653.

Trueman, Terry, *Stuck in Neutral.*

69

HarperCollins, 2000, 116pp. $16.98. ISBN: 0060285184. HarperCollins, 2001, 129pp. $6.99. ISBN: 0064472132. Recorded Books, 2000. $22.00. ISBN: 1402507100. Recorded Books, 2000. $29.00. CD. ISBN: 1402514867.

Web Site: <www.terrytrueman.com>
Subjects: Disabilities, Divorce, Emotional Problems, Family Problems, Fathers and Sons, Self-Identity
Genres: Realistic
Awards: 2001 Printz Honor
Lists: 2001 BBYA, 2001 QP
Levels: BL 6-10, K 7 up, PW 5 up, SLJ 5-9

Annotation: Fourteen-year-old Shawn is a genius locked inside a body incapacitated by cerebral palsy. Although he cannot move, he can hear and see and knows his father is thinking about ending his son's life because he thinks Shawn is in great pain when he has seizures. But Shawn loves the seizures as they allow his soul to leave his immobile body.

Booktalk: They think I can't hear them or understand what they are saying. My family says whatever they want to around me, even about me. And my sister and her friends talk girl talk around me all the time. The things they say when they think no one else is listening! Any teenage guy would love to hear these conversations. They don't know I can hear and understand them, and sometimes even see them when my eyes focus, during their slumber parties in the family room. They don't know that my body reacts just like any other guy and I have dreams of what would it be like to kiss a girl. One time during one of my seizures I was able to leave my body and watched myself holding hands with and a kissing a girl. It felt so real. I love my seizures – they free me to fly above everything and everyone.

Excerpt: Page 2 through first paragraph on page 5.

Curriculum Connections: Health, Science
Shawn is not able to communicate with his family due to his disability. Have students use library media center materials to research the various forms of communication that have been developed to help disabled people interact with other people.

Similar Titles:
Fleischman, Paul, *The Mind's Eye.* Holt, 1999, 108pp. $15.95. ISBN: 0805063145. Random House, 2001, 112pp. $5.50. ISBN: 0440229014.
Mikaelsen, Ben, *Petey.* Hyperion, 1998, 256pp. $15.95. ISBN: 0786804262. Hyperion, 2000, 256pp. $5.99. ISBN: 0786813369. Recorded Books, 2001. $37.00. ISBN: 0788745573.
Pincus, Dion, *Everything You Need to Know About Cerebral Palsy.* Rosen, 2000, 64pp. $18.95. ISBN: 0823929604.
Trueman, Terry, *Cruise Control.* HarperCollins, 2004, 160pp. $16.89. ISBN: 0066239613.
Woodruff, Joan Leslie, *The Shiloh Renewal.* Black Heron Press, 1998, 195pp. $22.95. ISBN: 0930773500.

70 Vance, Susanna, *Deep.*

Delacorte, 2003. $15.95. ISBN: 0385730578. Random House, 2005, 272pp. $5.50. ISBN: 0440238420.

Web Site: <www.susannavance.com>
Subjects: Alcoholism, Crime, Family Problems, Kidnapping, Murder, Occupations, Writing
Genres: International, Mystery, Realistic
Lists: 2004 BBYA
Levels: BL 7-10, K 7 up, PW 7 up, SLJ 6-8

Annotation: Seventeen-year-old Morgan leaves her alcoholic parents behind and sets out alone on the family sailboat at the same time 13-year-old Birdie's family arrives in the Caribbean. The girls are both kidnapped by a smooth-talking serial killer.

Booktalk: People say Birdie talks too much. They call her Birdie because she chirps aloud like a bird, all the time. Also, she is small for a 13-year-old because of her asthma. Her parents baby her and protect her, which is good sometimes, but not always. Birdie wants *something* to happen to her! She needs something to happen, or how else is she going to write an amazing book? Maybe amazing things will happen to her while her family is in Caribbean. Did I tell you that Birdie's parents are taking a year off from their regular jobs and they are going to live on an island? Birdie thinks it is going to be so much fun – maybe she will even meet some new friends. Well, Birdie will get an adventure to write about and then some when she meets the good-looking, but psycho, Nicholas. He offers to watch their luggage while her parents visit the shops near the wharf and then sails off with the luggage and Birdie on board his boat. Add Morgan, a girl who sails away with the family sailboat, leaving her parents behind, and you have quite a story when the paths of Nicholas, Birdie, and Morgan collide. Birdie may just have the plot for a murder mystery.

Excerpt: Page 33 through break on page 37.

Curriculum Connections: Math, Social Studies
Have students use library media center resources to choose and research a Caribbean destination, creating an itinerary and budget for a trip to their chosen island, based on the activities they would like to engage in.

Similar Titles:
Crowe, Carole, **Waiting for Dolphins.** Boyds Mills, 2003, 144pp. $16.95. ISBN: 1563978474. Boyds Mills, 2003, 144pp. $9.95. ISBN: 1590780736.
Lawrence, Ian, **Buccaneers.** The High Seas Trilogy. Delacorte, 2001, 244pp. $15.95. ISBN: 0385327366. Random House, 2003, 256pp. $5.50. ISBN: 044041671X.
Nixon, Joan Lowery, **Playing for Keeps.** Delacorte, 2001, 208pp. $15.95. ISBN: 0385327595. Random House, 2003, 208pp. $5.50. ISBN: 0440228670.
Taylor, Theodore, **Sweet Friday Island.** Harcourt, 1994, 192pp. $6.00. ISBN: 0152000127.
Taylor, Theodore, **Timothy of the Cay.** Harcourt, 1993, 176pp. $16.00. ISBN: 0152883584. HarperCollins, 1994, 145pp. $5.99. ISBN: 0380721198.

71. Whytock, Cherry, *My Cup Runneth Over: The Life of Angelica Cookson Potts.*

Simon & Schuster, 2003, 165pp. $14.95. ISBN: 0689865465. Simon & Schuster, 2004, 163pp. $5.99. ISBN: 0689865511.

Subjects: Cooking, Friendship, Mothers and Daughters, Occupations, Schools, Self-Esteem, Weight Control
Genres: Humor, International, Realistic
Lists: 2001 BBYA, 2001 QP
Levels: BL 6-9, K 5-8, PW 7 up, SLJ 7 up

Annotation: Fifteen-year-old Angel Potts loves eating what she cooks and bakes, but her ex-model mother doesn't approve of her daughter's large body or her desire to be a chef. Includes Angel's quirky recipes and her line drawings of friends and family.

Booktalk: How could a girl with the last name of Cookson Potts not become a famous chef someday? Angel is a natural in the kitchen – both when it comes to cooking and eating. That's the problem – she loves to eat as much as she loves to cook. She has to sample, sometimes with second and third helpings, the goodies she and the housekeeper Flossie create. This does not go over well with her whip thin, once a model mother who is constantly telling Angel to quit galumphing around the house. It is pretty hard to walk dainty when you are Angel's size. Let's just say she is never going to be a size 4 like her mother and Angel has pretty much accepted her size. The part she hasn't accepted is how bits of her body woggle about – especially the parts that runneth over the edges. A trip to the lingerie department solves that problem. Now if she can just figure out to get Adam to notice her!

Excerpt: (pbk.) From the break on page 8 through page 13.

Curriculum Connection: Health
Have the students use library media center cookbooks and other resources to create a menu for a healthy meal to accompany one of Angel's desserts.

Similar Titles:
Cabot, Meg, ***The Princess Diaries.*** The Princess Diaries Series. HarperCollins, 2000, 240pp. $16.89. ISBN: 0060292105. HarperTrophy, 2001, 304pp. $6.99. ISBN: 0380814021. Random House Audio, 2004. $38.00. ISBN: 0807206695. Random House Audio, 2004. $40.00. CD. ISBN: 0807211648.
Harrison, Lisi, ***The Clique.*** Little Brown, 2004, 220pp. $7.99. ISBN: 0316701297.
O'Connell, Tyne, ***Pulling Princes.*** The Calypso Chronicles. Bloomsbury, 2004, 223pp. $16.95. ISBN: 1582349576.

Rennison, Louise, ***Angus, Thongs, and Full-Frontal Snogging: Confession of Georgia Nicolson.*** HarperCollins, 2000, 256pp. $16.89. ISBN: 006028871X. HarperTempest, 2001, 272pp. $6.99. ISBN: 0064472272. Recorded Books, 2004. $14.99. ISBN: 1402508662.

Whytock, Cherry, ***My Scrumptious Scottish Dumplings: The Life of Angelica Cookson Potts.*** Simon & Schuster, 2004, 176pp. $14.95. ISBN: 068986549X.

Wilhelm, Doug, *The Revealers.* — 72

Farrar, Straus & Giroux, 2003, 207pp. $16.00. ISBN: 0374382556. Farrar, Straus & Giroux, 2005, 224pp. $6.95. ISBN: 0374462437.

Web Site: <www.the-revealers.com/meet-doug>
Subjects: Bullies, Friendship, Prejudices, Schools, Writing
Genres: Multicultural, Realistic
Levels: BL 4-6, K 5-8, PW 5 up, SLJ 5-7

Annotation: Three seventh grade students fight back against the school bullies by creating an online forum, called The Revealer, to let other students know what has been happening to them. The other students add their own bullying stories and expose the level of the problem in the school.

Booktalk: Did you ever notice how other people tend to ignore the mistreatment of the "not so cool" kids in school, especially the guy geeks and the girls who look different? There are various ways to deal with bullies and the middle schoolers in this book have come up with their own unique way of doing so. Elliott, who uses his knowledge of predatory dinosaurs to stay away from the bullies; Catalina, whose exotic Filipino looks make her a favorite target for the preppy girls; and Russell, the punching bag for the neighborhood bully, join forces to fight back. They use their brains instead of their brawn and create the Darkland Revealer – an online forum where kids can share their stories. More and more students share their stories of how they have been made fun of and been the target for the school bullies. The bullies can't hide their behavior anymore. It is out in the open, all on the school intranet for everyone to read, and even the principal has to sit up and take notice.

Excerpt: Pages 91 through 93.

Curriculum Connection: Social Studies
Have students use library media resources to discover how bullying is addressed in articles and other materials about student interaction in schools. Then elicit a class discussion as to how the students in *The Revealers* handled the situation, addressing whether or not any of these options are viable in their own school.

Similar Titles:

Brooks, Kevin, ***Kissing the Rain.*** Scholastic, 2004, 336pp. $16.95. ISBN: 043957742X. Scholastic, 2005, 384pp. $7.99. ISBN: 0439577438.

Howe, James, ***The Misfits.*** Atheneum, 2001, 288pp. $16.00. ISBN: 0689839553. Simon & Schuster, 2004, 274pp. $5.99. ISBN: 0689839561. Full Cast Audio, 2002. $21.95. ISBN: 1932076115. Full Cast Audio, 2003. $31.00. CD. ISBN: 1932076220.

Huser, Glen, ***Stitches.*** Groundwood Books, 2003, 224pp. $15.95. ISBN: 0888995539. Groundwood Books, 2005, 200pp. $9.95. ISBN: 0888995784.

Myers, Walter Dean, ***Scorpions.*** HarperCollins, 1988, 224pp. $16.89. ISBN: 0060243651. HarperCollins, 1996, 224pp. $5.99. ISBN: 0064406237.

Spinelli, Jerry, ***Wringer.*** HarperCollins, 1997, 228pp. $16.89. ISBN: 0060249145. HarperCollins, 2004, 227pp. $6.50. ISBN: 0060592826. Recorded Books, 1998. $35.00. ISBN: 0788717987. Recorded Books, 2000. $39.00. CD. ISBN: 0788747428.

---

73 Williams, Maiya, *The Golden Hour.*

Abrams, 2004, 272pp. $16.95. ISBN: 0810948230.

Web Site: <www.maiyawilliams.com>
Subjects: African Americans, Brothers and Sisters, Elderly, Friendship, Grieving, Journeys, Time Travel
Genres: Fantasy, Historical, Multicultural
Levels: BL 4-8, K 5-7, PW 4-9, SLJ 5-8

Annotation: After their mother dies, Rowan and Nina are sent to spend the summer with their eccentric great aunts in northern Maine. With the twins Xanthe and Xavier, Rowan travels back in time to the French Revolution where they think they will find Nina.

Booktalk: Rowan and Nina are shipped off to spend the summer with two great aunts who they don't even know. All the way around this little town in Maine is strange. It's in a time warp or something. Rowan is sure that his eccentric great aunts aren't telling quite all of the truth when they say they collect and sell antiques. Sure, the things stuck in every nook and cranny of their house are from different time periods, but they don't look old. They look brand new, many of them without a scratch on them. It's like the two old ladies dropped into different time periods and just picked up something to take back with them, kind of like time-traveling tourists. Rowan is positive that there is something odd going on in this town. And he thinks it has something to do with the old hotel his aunt keeps telling him to stay away from. Maybe it was time Rowan takes a look at what is inside that old hotel. But Nina had the same idea and got there first and now she is missing.

Excerpt: Page 22, second paragraph, to break at the bottom of page 27.

Curriculum Connection: Social Studies

Rowan, Xanthe, and Xavier time travel to the French Revolution. Rowan meets and talks with both Louis XVI and Queen Marie Antoinette. Have students use library media center materials to research this couple and their role in the French Revolution, creating a list of questions they would like to ask Louis XVI and Marie Antoinette.

Similar Titles:

Cooney, Caroline B., ***Both Sides of Time.*** Bantam Doubleday Dell, 1997, 210pp. $5.50. ISBN: 0440219329.

L'Engle, Madeleine, ***An Acceptable Time.*** The O'Keefe Family Series. Farrar, Straus & Giroux, 1989, 343pp. $18.00. ISBN: 0374300275. Bantam Doubleday Dell, 1990, 343pp. $5.99. ISBN: 0440208149.

Lunn, Janet, ***The Root Cellar.*** Penguin, 1996, 229pp. $5.99. ISBN: 0140380361.

Paulsen, Gary, ***The Transall Saga.*** Bantam Doubleday Dell, 1999, 248pp. $5.99. ISBN: 0440219760.

Reiss, Kathryn, ***PaperQuake: A Puzzle.*** Harcourt, 2002, 288pp. $6.00. ISBN: 015216782X.

74

Zeises, Lara M., *Contents Under Pressure.*

Delacorte, 2004. 244pp. $15.95. ISBN: 0385730470.

Web Site: <www.zeisgeist.com>
Subjects: Brothers and Sisters, Family Problems, Relationships, Sexuality
Genres: Realistic
Levels: BL 6-9, K 6-9, PW 7 up, SLJ 7-10, V 5-8

Annotation: Fourteen-year-old Lucy is dismayed by the dissolution of childhood friendships, confused about her brother Jack's return from college with his pregnant girlfriend, and scared by her emotional and physical responses to her boyfriend.

Booktalk: Lucy literally runs into Tobin Scacheri, one of the coolest Junior guys. The problem is, this isn't the first time she has been physical with him. You see, she actually jumped on his back at the football game last weekend, wrapping her legs around his waist. How embarrassing is that? He just smiled at her when she tried to explain that she thought he was her older brother. After that incident you'd think he would stay as far away from her as possible. But instead, Tobin helps her up off the hallway floor and asks her out. Before she knows it, Lucy is the girlfriend of one of the most popular boys in school. But Lucy's home life isn't as wonderful as her relationship with Tobin. She hates sharing her room with her brother Jack's pregnant girlfriend Hannah, that is until Hannah begins to answer Lucy's questions about how to handle her relationship with Tobin. She knows she doesn't want to be like her friend Tabitha and go all the way with the first guy she gets serious with, but how is she supposed to deal with the feelings she has inside? What's okay and what isn't? How do you tell a guy no and still keep him?

Excerpt: Page 3, first full paragraph, to break on page 7.

Curriculum Connection: Health
Have students use library media center resources to research dating rituals in the past and in different cultural groups today. Using this knowledge, have students break up into groups and brainstorm alternative dialogs that could occur between Lucy and Tobin as they decide how to set the boundaries on their physical relationship.

Similar Titles:
Fredericks, Mariah, ***The True Meaning of Cleavage.*** Atheneum, 2003, 224pp. $15.95. ISBN: 0689850921. Simon & Schuster, 2004, 240pp. $6.99. ISBN: 0689869584.
Mackler, Carolyn, ***Love and Other Four Letter Words.*** Bantam Doubleday Dell, 2002, 256pp. $5.99. ISBN: 044022831X.
McWilliams, Kelly, ***Doormat.*** Random House, 2004, 128pp. $15.95. ISBN: 038573168X.
Moriarty, Jaclyn, ***Year of Secret Assignments.*** Scholastic, 2004, 240pp. $16.95. ISBN: 0439498813. Scholastic, 2005, 352pp. $6.99. ISBN: 0439498821.
Sones, Sonya, ***What My Mother Doesn't Know.*** Simon & Schuster, 2002, 272pp. $17.00. ISBN: 0689841140. Simon & Schuster, 2003, 272pp. $6.99. ISBN: 0689855532.

75 Zindel, Paul, *Night of the Bat.*

Hyperion, 2001, 129pp. $15.99. ISBN: 0786803401. Hyperion, 2003, 144pp. $5.99. ISBN: 0786812265.

Subjects: Animals, Bats, Death, Fathers and Sons, Violence
Genres: Horror, International
Lists: 2002 QP
Levels: BL 6-9, K 7-9, PW 5-9, SLJ 6-10, V 6-9

Annotation: Wanting to prove himself to his biologist father, 15-year-old Jake joins his father's research team in the Brazilian rainforest and discovers that a huge mutant vampire bat is killing the research team members. When his father is injured, Jake has to fight the bloodthirsty bat alone.

Booktalk: Jake stuffed the peanut butter cookies from the in-flight dinner into his backpack and headed down the aisle. He wanted nothing more than to get off of this plane. People were still looking at him oddly after the stewardess had to wake him from his nightmare. He joked that he dreamt his allowance had been cut. He wasn't about to tell them what he actually dreamt. He rubbed his hand across his mouth as he thought about the feeling of its fur on his face, the sharp little teeth that bit into his lips, and the legs and wings trying to crawl into his mouth. But, it was the realization that in his dream there was a tiny head inside his mouth biting him that brought out the scream that startled everyone. Jake was sure his nightmare was just because he had spent too much time reading about the vampire bats in the Amazon. But, Jake had better get it together quickly because he was getting off a plane in Brazil and headed into the rain forest to join his father and his research team who are working with vampire bats.

Excerpt: Page 12, first full paragraph, through page 14.

Curriculum Connection: Science
Have students use library media center materials to research vampire bats, where they live, how they feed, and why they are so feared by man.

Similar Titles:
Houghton, Sarah, ***Bloodsuckers: Bats, Bugs, and Other Bloodthirsty Creatures.*** Capstone, 48pp, 2003. $22.60. ISBN: 0736827897.
Zindel, Paul, ***Loch.*** HarperCollins, 1994, 209pp. $15.89. ISBN: 0060245433. Disney Press, 1995, 224pp. $4.95. ISBN: 0786810998.
Zindel, Paul, ***Raptor.*** Disney Press, 1999, 176pp. $4.99. ISBN: 0786812249.
Zindel, Paul, ***Rats.*** Disney Press, 2000, 176pp. $4.99. ISBN: 0786812257.
Zindel, Paul, ***Reef of Death.*** HarperCollins, 1998, 192pp. $15.95. ISBN: 0060247282. Hyperion, 1999, 192pp. $5.99. ISBN: 0786813091.

SECTION 6

Indices

For ease of access, the numbers in the indices refer to the entry number, rather than to a page number.

A. Author

Allende, Isabel, *Kingdom of the Golden Dragon* 1
Almond, David, *Skellig* 2
Bell, Hilari, *The Goblin Wood* 3
Bell, Hilari, *The Wizard Test* 4
Bruchac, Joseph, *Sacajawea: The Story of Bird Woman and the
  Lewis and Clark Expedition* 5
Carman, Patrick, *The Dark Hills Divide* 6
Cassidy, Cathy, *Dizzy* 7
Clark, Clara Gillow, *Hill Hawk Hattie* 8
Clinton, Cathryn, *A Stone in My Hand* 9
Cofer, Judith Ortiz, *Call Me Maria* 10
Cohn, Rachel, *The Steps* 11
Cooper, Ilene, *Sam I Am* 12
Couloumbis, Audrey, *Getting Near to Baby* 13
Creech, Sharon, *Granny Torrelli Makes Soup* 14
Creedon, Catherine, *Blue Wolf* 15
Curtis, Christopher Paul, *Bud, Not Buddy* 16
Curtis, Christopher Paul, *The Watsons Go to Birmingham–1963* 17
D'Adamo, Francesco, *Iqbal* 18
Danticat, Edwidge, *Behind the Mountains: The Diary of Celiane Esperance* ..19

De Guzman, Michael, *Beekman's Big Deal* 20
Deak, Erzsi and Kristin Embry-Litchman, eds., *Period Pieces:
   Stories for Girls* 21
Dodd, Quentin, *The Princess of Neptune* 22
Dorros, Arthur, *Under the Sun* 23
Durbin, William, *The Darkest Evening* 24
Edwards, Julie Andrews and Emma Walton Hamilton, *Dragon:
   Hound of Honor* 25
Farmer, Nancy, *The House of the Scorpion* 26
Farmer, Nancy, *The Sea of Trolls* 27
Feinstein, John, *Last Shot* 28
Fisher, Catherine, *The Oracle Betrayed* 29
Frank, E.R., *Friction* 30
Funke, Cornelia, *The Thief Lord* 31
Gaiman, Neil, *Coraline* 32
Gantos, Jack, *Joey Pigza Loses Control* 33
Giff, Patricia Reilly, *Pictures of Hollis Woods* 34
Greene, Bette, *I've Already Forgotten Your Name, Philip Hall!* 35
Griffin, Peni R., *11,000 Years Lost* 36
Grossman, David, *Duel* 37
Harlow, Joan Hiatt, *Shadows on the Sea* 38
Hesse, Karen, *Aleutian Sparrow* 39
Hiaasen, Carl, *Hoot* 40
Hobbs, Will, *Wild Man Island* 41
Holm, Jennifer L., *Boston Jane: The Claim* 42
Holm, Jennifer L., *The Creek* 43
Holt, Kimberly Willis, *My Louisiana Sky* 44
Hooper, Mary, *Petals in the Ashes* 45
Jarvis, Robin, *The Final Reckoning* 46
Jarvis, Robin, *The Thorn Ogres of Hagwood* 47
Jinks, Catherine, *Pagan's Vows* 48
Kerr, M.E., *Snakes Don't Miss Their Mothers* 49
Lowry, Lois, *Gathering Blue* 50
Lynch, Chris, *The Gravedigger's Cottage* 51
Martin, Ann M., *Here Today* 52
Mead, Alice, *Year of No Rain* 53
Myers, Anna, *Stolen by the Sea* 54
Myers, Walter Dean, *A Time to Love: Stories from the Old Testament* 55
Naidoo, Beverley, *The Other Side of Truth* 56
Nelson, Theresa, *Ruby Electric* 57
Paver, Michelle, *Wolf Brother* 58
Pierce, Tamora, *Alanna: The First Adventure* 59
Pratchett, Terry, *The Amazing Maurice and His Educated Rodents* 60
Pratchett, Terry, *A Hat Full of Sky: The Continuing Adventures of Tiffany Aching
   and the Wee Free Men* 61

Rinaldi, Ann, *Nine Days a Queen: The Short Life and Reign of Lady Jane Grey* . .62
Roberts, Willo Davis, *Rebel* 63
Sage, Angie, *Magyk* 64
Skurzynski, Gloria, *Virtual War* 65
Sleator, William, *Oddballs* 66
Spinelli, Jerry, *Loser* 67
Tashjian, Janet, *Multiple Choice* 68
Trueman, Terry, *Stuck in Neutral* 69
Vance, Susanna, *Deep* 70
Whytock, Cherry, *My Cup Runneth Over: The Life of Angelica Cookson Potts* . .71
Wilhelm, Doug, *The Revealers* 72
Williams, Maiya, *The Golden Hour* 73
Zeises, Lara M., *Contents Under Pressure* 74
Zindel, Paul, *Night of the Bat* 75

B. Authors, Similar Titles

Adams, Richard, *Tales from Watership Down* 60
Adams, Richard, *Watership Down* 60
Agell, Charlotte, *Welcome Home or Someplace Like It* 38
Al-Windawi, Thura, *Thura's Diary: My Life in Wartime Iraq* 9
Alexander, Sally Hobart, *Do You Remember the Color Blue?:*
   Questions Children Ask About Being Blind 14
Allende, Isabel, *City of the Beasts* 1
Almond, David, *Counting Stars* 2
Almond, David, *The Fire Eaters* 2
Almond, David, *Heaven Eyes* 2
Almond, David, *Secret Heart* 2
Alvarez, Julia, *Before We Were Free* 19
Armistead, John, *The Return of Gabriel* 17
Armstrong, Jennifer, *The Kindling* 65
Armstrong, Jennifer, *Shattered: Stories of Children and War* 9
Armstrong, William H., *Sounder* 16
Avi, *Blue Heron* 57
Avi, *The True Confessions of Charlotte Doyle* 8
Ayer, Katherine, *Under Copp's Hill* 14
Baglio, Ben M., *Owl in the Office* 49
Baillett, Blue, *Chasing Vermeer* 34
Barker, Clive, *Abarat* 46
Barron, T.A., *The Ancient One* 15
Barron, T.A., *The Lost Years of Merlin* 64
Bauer, Joan, *Stand Tall* 57
Beals, Melba Patillo, *Warriors Don't Cry* 17
Bell, Hilari, *A Matter of Profit* 3
Bell, William, *Forbidden City: A Novel of Modern Day China* 1

Benderly, Beryl Lieff, *Jason's Miracle: A Hanukkah Story* 12
Biesanz, Mavis Hiltunen, *Helmi Mavis: A Finnish-American Girlhood* 24
Bjork, Christina, *Vendela in Venice* 31
Blackstone, Margaret and Elissa Haden Guest, *Girl Stuff:
   A Survival Guide to Growing Up* 21
Block, Joel D., *Stepliving for Teens: Getting Along with
   Stepparents and Siblings* 11
Bloor, Edward, *Tangerine* 14
Blume, Judy, *Are You There God? It's Me, Margaret* 30
Blume, Judy, *It's Not the End of the World* 57
Bode, N.E., *Anybodies* 51
Bowermaster, Jon, *Aleutian Adventure: Kayaking in the Birthplace
   of the Winds* 39
Bradby, Maria, *Some Friend* 35
Branford, Henrietta, *Fated Sky* 27
Breuilly, Elizabeth, *Religions of the World: The Illustrated Guide to Origins,
   Beliefs, Traditions and Festivals* 7
Brooks, Bruce, *The Moves Make the Man* 28
Brooks, Bruce, *What Hearts* 57
Brooks, Kevin, *Kissing the Rain* 72
Browning, Robert, *The Pied Piper of Hamlin* 60
Bryant, Ann, *One Mom Too Many* 11
Byars, Betsy, *Summer of the Swans* 44
Byng, Georgia, *Molly Moon's Incredible Book of Hypnotism* 32
Cabot, Meg, *The Princess Diaries* 71
Cadnum, Michael, *Book of the Lion* 25
Cadnum, Michael, *Daughter of the Wind* 27
Cadnum, Michael, *The Leopard Sword* 48
Card, Orson Scott, *Ender's Game* 26
Carmi, Daniella, *Samir and Yonatan* 37
Challoner, Jack, *Hurricane and Tornado* 54
Cisneros, Sandra, *The House on Mango Street* 30
Clark, Clara Gillow, *Hattie on Her Way* 8
Cleary, Beverly, *Dear Mr. Henshaw* 16
Clements, Andrew, *Frindle* 67
Clements, Andrew, *The Last Holiday Concert* 67
Clements, Andrew, *Things Not Seen* 22
Clements, Andrew, *A Week in the Woods* 41
Cofer, Judith Ortiz, *The Meaning of Consuelo* 10
Cofer, Judith Ortiz, *Silent Dancing: A Partial Remembrance of a
   Puerto Rican Childhood* 10
Colfer, Eoin, *Artemis Fowl* 64
Colfer, Eoin, *The Supernaturalist* 26
Collins, Suzanne, *Gregor the Overlander and the Prophecy of Bane* ...47
Cooney, Caroline B., *Both Sides of Time* 73

Cooney, Caroline B., *For All Time* 29
Cooney, Caroline B., *Goddess of Yesterday* 29
Corder, Zizou, *Lionboy* 58
Coville, Bruce, *Into the Land of the Unicorns* 6
Craig, Steve, *Sportswriting: A Beginner's Guide* 28
Creech, Sharon, *Absolutely Normal Chaos* 35
Creech, Sharon, *Ruby Holler* 34
Creech, Sharon, *Walk Two Moons* 16
Crew, Linda, *Fire on the Wind* 8
Crowe, Carole, *Waiting for Dolphins* 70
Curry, Jane Louise, *The Egyptian Box* 29
Cushman, Karen, *Catherine, Called Birdy* 48
Cushman, Karen, *Matilda Bone* 48
Dahl, Roald, *The BFG* 32
Dahl, Roald, *The Wonderful Story of Henry Sugar and Six More* 66
Danziger, Paula, *The Divorce Express* 57
Danziger, Paula, *There's a Bat in Bunk Five* 7
Danziger, Paula, *This Place Has No Atmosphere* 20
Davis, Kenneth C., *Don't Know Much About Kings and Queens of England* 62
Davis, Ossie, *Just Like Martin* 17
De Guzman, Michael, *Melonhead* 20
Deuker, Carl, *Night Hoops* 28
DiCamillo, Kate, *Because of Winn Dixie* 52
DiCamillo, Kate, *Tale of Despereaux: Being the Story of a Mouse, a Princess, Some Soup, and a Spool of Thread* 47
DiCamillo, Kate, *Tiger Rising* 13
Dickinson, Peter, *A Bone From a Dry Sea* 36
Dickinson, Peter, *The Kin: Suth's Story* 36
Dodd, Quentin, *Beatnik Rutabagas From Beyond the Stars* 22
Duane, Diane, *So You Want to Be a Wizard* 4
Duane, Diane, *A Wizard Alone* 64
Duncan, Lois, *Gallows Hill* 61
Dunkle, Clare B., *Close Kin* 3
Dunkle, Clare B., *The Hollow Kingdom* 3
DuPrau, Jeanne, *The People of Sparks* 6
Durbin, William, *The Journal of Otto Peltonen: A Finnish Immigrant: Hibbing Minnesota, 1905* 24
Durbin, William, *Song of Sampo Lake* 24
Elish, Dan, *Born Too Short: The Confessions of an Eighth-Grade Basket Case* 66
Ellis, Deborah, *The Breadwinner* 56
Emmer, E.R., *The Dolphin Project* 37
Ende, Michael, *The Neverending Story* 6
Ende, Michael, *The Night of Wishes* 6
Ewing, Lynne, *The Talisman* 29

Farmer, Nancy, *The Eye, the Ear, and the Arm* 53
Farmer, Nancy, *A Girl Named Disaster* 53
Feinstein, Edward, *Tough Questions Jews Ask: A Young Adult's Guide to Building a Jewish Life* 12
Filipovic, Zlata, *Zlata's Diary: A Child's Life in Sarajevo* 23
Fireside, Harvey, *Young People from Bosnia Talk about War* 23
Fisher, Susan Staples, *Shabanu: Daughter of the Wind* 18
Fleischman, Paul, *The Mind's Eye* 69
Fleischman, Sid, *The Whipping Boy* 16
Fredericks, Mariah, *The True Meaning of Cleavage* 74
Friesen, Gayle, *Losing Forever* 11
Funke, Cornelia, *The Dragon Rider* 32
Funke, Cornelia, *Inkheart* 31
Gabrielpillai, Matilda, *Bosnia and Herzegovina* 23
Gaiman, Neil, *The Wolves in the Walls* 32
Gantos, Jack, *Heads or Tails: Stories from the Sixth Grade* 33
Gantos, Jack, *Joey Pigza Swallowed the Key* 33
Gantos, Jack, *What Would Joey Do?* 33
Garland, Sherry, *Silent Storm* 54
George, Jean Craighead, *Case of the Missing Cutthroats* 40
George, Jean Craighead, *Frightful's Mountain* 49
George, Jean Craighead, *Julie* 58
George, Jean Craighead, *Julie of the Wolves* 41
George, Jean Craighead, *There's an Owl in the Shower* 40
Goldberg, Jan, *Perfectionism: What's Bad About Being Too Good?* 68
Goldin, Barbara Diamond, *Journeys with Elijah: Eight Tales of the Prophet* .55
Gravelle, Karen, Jennifer Gravelle and Debbie Palen, *The Period Book: Everything You Don't Want to Ask (But Need to Know)* 21
Gray, Luli, *Timespinners* 36
Greenblatt, Miriam, *Elizabeth I and Tudor England* 62
Greene, Bette, *Get on Out of Here, Philip Hall!* 35
Greene, Bette, *Philip Hall Likes Me, I Reckon Maybe* 35
Greene, Bette, *Summer of My German Soldier* 38
Griese, Arnold A., *A Wind Is Not a River* 39
Griffiths, Andy, *The Day My Butt Went Psycho* 66
Haddix, Margaret Peterson, *Among the Hidden* 50
Hahn, Mary Downing, *Dead Man in Indian Creek* 43
Hahn, Mary Downing, *The Gentleman Outlaw and Me–Eli* 8
Hahn, Mary Downing, *Stepping on the Cracks* 38
Hapka, Cathy, *Oasis* 36
Harlow, Joan Hiatt, *Joshua's Song* 18
Harrar, George, *Not as Crazy as I Seem* 68
Harrison, Lisi, *The Clique* 71
Hautman, Pete, *Hole in the Sky* 50
Herzog, Brad, *The Hoopmania: The Book of Basketball History and Trivia* ...28

Hesse, Karen, *Out of the Dust* 16
Hesser, Terry Spencer, *Kissing Doorknobs* 68
Hobbs, Will, *Ghost Canoe* 42
Hobbs, Will, *The Maze* 40
Hodge, Merle, *For the Life of Leatitia* 19
Holm, Jennifer L., *Boston Jane: An Adventure* 42
Holm, Jennifer L., *Boston Jane: Wilderness Days* 42
Holm, Jennifer L., *Our Only May Amelia* 24
Holt Kimberly Willis, *When Zachary Beaver Came to Town* 52
Holyoke, Nancy, *Yikes!: A Smart Girl's Guide to Surviving Tricky,
    Sticky, Icky Situations* 21
Hooper, Mary, *At the Sign of the Sugared Plum* 45
Horowitz, Anthony, *Point Blank* 65
Horvath, Polly, *Everything on a Waffle* 51
Hoshikawa, Jun, *Beringia: Bridge of Spirits* 58
Houghton, Sarah, *Bloodsuckers: Bats, Bugs, and Other Bloodthirsty
    Creatures* 75
Howe, James, *The Misfits* 72
Howe, Norma, *Blue Avenger Cracks the Code* 31
Hunter, Elrose, *The Story Atlas of the Bible* 55
Hunter, Erin, *Into the Wild* 47
Hunter, Molly, *The Walking Stones* 7
Hurwitz, Jane, *Coping in a Blended Family* 11
Huser, Glen, *Stitches* 72
Hussein, Ikram, *Teenage Refugees from Somalia Speak Out* 56
Hyman, Bruce M., *Obsessive Compulsive Disorder* 68
Ives, David, *Monsieur Eek* 51
Jacques, Brian, *Martin the Warrior* 46
Jacques, Brian, *Redwall* 6
Jarvis, Robin, *The Alchemist's Cat* 60
Jarvis, Robin, *The Crystal Prison* 46
Jarvis, Robin, *The Dark Portal* 46
Jiang, Ji-Li, *Red Scarf Girl: A Memoir of the Cultural Revolution* 9
Jinks, Catherine, *Pagan in Exile* 48
Jinks, Catherine, *Pagan's Crusade* 48
Jones, Diana Wynne, *Cart and Cwidder* 36
Jones, Diana Wynne, *The Spellcoats* 58
Jones, Martha Tannery, *Terror from the Gulf: A Hurricane in Galveston* 54
Jukes, Mavis, *It's a Girl Thing: Straight Talk About First Bras,
    First Periods, and Your Changing Body* 21
Kehret, Peg, *Danger at the Fair* 63
Kehret, Peg, *Shelter Dogs: Amazing Stories of Adopted Strays* 49
Kehret, Peg, *Stranger Next Door* 20
Kielburger, Craig, *Free the Children: A Young Man Fights Against
    Child Labor and Proves That Children Can Change the World* 18

Kindl, Patrice, *Owl In Love* 15
Koller, Jackie French, *The Wizard's Apprentice* 64
Konigsburg, E.L., *From the Mixed-Up Files of Mrs. Basil E. Frankweiler* 20
Konigsburg, E.L., *Silent to the Bone* 68
Konigsburg, E.L., *A View from Saturday* 52
Korman, Gordon, *No More Dead Dogs* 22
Krisher, Trudy B., *Kinship* 7
Kuklin, Susan, *Iqbal Masih and the Crusaders Against Child Slavery* 18
Lasky, Kathryn, *An American Spring: Sofia's Immigrant Diary,
  The North End of Boston, 1903* 14
Lasky, Kathryn, *The Capture* 47
Lasky, Kathryn, *Elizabeth I: Red Rose of the House of Tudor, England, 1544* ...62
Lawrence, Ian, *Buccaneers* 70
Layne, Steven L., *This Side of Paradise* 26
L'Engle, Madeleine, *An Acceptable Time* 73
L'Engle, Madeleine, *A Swiftly Tilting Planet* 26
L'Engle, Madeleine, *Troubling a Star* 43
Le Guin, Ursula K., *A Wizard of Earthsea* 4
Lee, Harper, *To Kill a Mockingbird* 30
Lisle, Janet Taylor, *The Art of Keeping Cool* 38
Lowry, Lois, *The Giver* 50
Lowry, Lois, *The Messenger* 50
Lowry, Lois, *Silent Boy* 2
Lunn, Janet, *The Root Cellar* 73
MacDonald, Margaret Reed, *Ghost Stories of the Pacific Northwest* 42
Mackler, Carolyn, *Love and Other Four Letter Words* 74
Manushkin, Fran, *Daughters of Fire: Heroines of the Bible* 55
Margeson, Susan M., *Viking* 27
Martin, Ann M., *Belle Teale* 52
Martin, Ann M., *A Corner of the Universe* 51
Matthews, Kezi, *John Riley's Daughter* 44
McDaniel, Lurlene, *The Girl Death Left Behind* 13
McKillip, Patricia A., *The Forgotten Beasts of Eld* 4
McKissack, Patricia C., *Nzingha: Warrior Queen of Matamba,
  Angola, Africa, 1595.* 53
McKissack, Patricia C., *The Royal Kingdoms of Ghana, Mali and Songhay:
Life in Medieval Africa* 53
McLaren, Clemence, *Waiting for Odysseus* 29
McWilliams, Kelly, *Doormat* 74
Meyer, Caroline, *Mary, Bloody Mary* 62
Meyer, Caroline, *Patience, Princess Catherine* 62
Meyer, Donald J., *Views from Our Shoes: Growing Up with a
  Brother or Sister with Special Needs* 44
Meyer, Stephanie H., ed., *Teen Ink: A Collection of Short Stories,
  Art and Photography* 34

Mikaelsen, Ben, *Petey* .69
Mikaelsen, Ben, *Touching Spirit Bear* .41
Miklowitz, Gloria D., *The Enemy Has a Face* .9
Miller-Lachmann, Lyn, *Once Upon a Cuento* .10
Mohr, Nicholasa, *Going Home* .10
Moriarty, Jaclyn, *Year of Secret Assignments* .74
Morris, Gerald, *Parsifal's Page* .25
Morrison, Jaydene, *Coping with ADD/ADHD (Attention Deficit Disorder/Attention Deficit Hyperactivity Disorder)* .33
Morrison, Toni, *Remember: The Journey to School Integration* .17
Mosatche, Harriet S. and Karen Unger, *Too Old For This, Too Young For That!: Your Survival Guide For the Middle-School Years* .21
Murphy, Patricia J., *Nigeria* .56
Murphy, Rita, *Black Angels* .17
Myers, Walter Dean, *Scorpions* .72
Na, An, *Step From Heaven* .15
Naidoo, Beverley, *Chain of Fire* .56
Naidoo, Beverley, *Journey to Jo'burg: A South African Story* .53
Naidoo, Beverley, *No Turning Back: A Novel of South Africa* .56
Naidoo, Beverley, *Out of Bounds: Seven Stories of Conflict and Hope* .9
Napoli, Donna Jo, *Daughter of Venice* .31
Napoli, Donna Jo, *For the Love of Venice* .31
Naylor, Phyllis Reynolds, *Simply Alice* .30
Neale, Jonathan, *Himalaya* .1
Nicholson, Michael, *Sarajevo: Natasha's Story* .23
Nicolson, Cynthia Pratt, *Hurricane!* .54
Nixon, Joan Lowery, *Playing for Keeps* .70
Nixon, Joan Lowery, *Shadowmaker* .63
North, Sterling, *Rascal* .49
Nye, Naomi Shihab, *19 Varieties of Gazelle: Poems of the Middle East* .37
Nye, Naomi Shihab, *Habibi* .37
O'Brien, Robert C., *Mrs. Frisby and the Rats of NIMH* .46
O'Connell, Tyne, *Pulling Princes* .71
O'Dell, Scott, *Island of the Blue Dolphins* .13
O'Dell, Scott, *Streams to the River, River to the Sea: A Novel of Sacajawea* .5
Oldfield, Pamela, *The Great Plague: The Diary of Alice Payton, London 1665-1666* .45
Osa, Nancy, *Cuba 15* .19
Park, Barbara, *The Graduation of Jake Moon* .34
Park, Linda Sue, *My Name Was Keoko* .15
Parker, David L., *Stolen Dreams: Portraits of Working Children* .18
Paterson, Katherine, *Bridge to Terabithia* .13
Paterson, Katherine, *The Great Gilly Hopkins* .34
Paterson, Katherine, *A Midnight Clear: Family Christmas Stories* .12
Patneaude, David, *Thin Wood Walls* .39

Paulsen, Gary, *Harris and Me: A Summer Remembered* 66
Paulsen, Gary, *Hatchet* 41
Paulsen, Gary, *The Tent: A Parable in One Sitting* 55
Paulsen, Gary, *The Transall Saga* 73
Peck, Richard, *A Long Way From Chicago* 14
Peck, Richard, *A Year Down Yonder* 51
Philbrick, Rodman, *The Last Book in the Universe* 26
Picard, Barbara Leonie, *Tales of the Norse Gods* 27
Pierce, Tamora, *In the Hand of the Goddess* 59
Pierce, Tamora, *Lady Knight* 59
Pierce, Tamora, *Lioness Rampant* 59
Pierce, Tamora, *Page* 59
Pierce, Tamora, *Squire* 25
Pierce, Tamora, *Street Magic* 4
Pierce, Tamora, *Wolf-Speaker* 58
Pierce, Tamora, *The Woman Who Rides Like a Man* 59
Pincus, Dion, *Everything You Need to Know About Cerebral Palsy* 69
Pinkwater, Daniel M., *5 Novels: Alan Mendelsohn, The Boy From Mars, Slaves of Spiegel, The Last Guru, The Snarkout Boys and The Avocado of Death* 22
Pinkwater, Daniel M., *Looking for Bobowicz: A Hoboken Chicken Story* 20
Polikoff, Barbara Garland, *Why Does the Coqui Sing?* 10
Pratchett, Terry, *The Bromeliad Trilogy: Truckers, Diggers, and Wings* 22
Pratchett, Terry, *Equal Rites* 61
Pratchett, Terry, *The Wee Free Men* 61
Pratchett, Terry, *Witches Abroad* 61
Pratchett, Terry, *Wyrd Sisters* 61
Prince, Maggie, *House on Hound Hill* 45
Pullman, Phillip, *The Golden Compass* 50
Pullman, Phillip, *The Ruby in the Smoke* 45
Quinn, Patricia O. and Judith M. Stern, *Putting On the Brakes: Young People's Guide to Understanding Attention Deficit Hyperactivity Disorder* 33
Reiss, Kathryn, *PaperQuake: A Puzzle* 73
Rennison, Louise, *Angus, Thongs, and Full-Frontal Snogging: Confession of Georgia Nicolson* 71
Richardson, Bill, *After Hamelin* 60
Rinaldi, Ann, *Girl in Blue* 8
Ringstad, Muriel, *Eye of the Changer: Northwest Indian Tale* 42
Roberts, Willo Davis, *Buddy is a Stupid Name for a Girl* 63
Roberts, Willo Davis, *Scared Stiff* 43
Roberts, Willo Davis, *Twisted Summer* 63
Robinson, Barbara, *The Best Christmas Pageant Ever* 12
Robinson, Barbara, *The Best School Year Ever* 67

Rockwell, Thomas, *How to Eat Fried Worms* 67
Rogers, Lisa Waller, *Great Storm: The Hurricane Diary of T.J. King,
　Galveston, Texas, 1900* 54
Roop, Peter, *Sacagawea: Girl of the Shining Mountains* 5
Rosen, Michael, *Elijah's Angel: A Story for Chanukah and Christmas* 12
Rowling, J.K., *Harry Potter and the Sorcerer's Stone* 64
Sachar, Louis, *The Boy Who Lost His Face* 67
Sachar, Louis, *Holes* 43
Schmidt, Thomas and Jeremy Schmidt, *Saga of Lewis and Clark:
　Into the Uncharted West* 5
Sevander, Mayme, *They Took My Father: Finnish Americans in Stalin's
　Russia* 24
Shearer, Alex, *The Great Blue Yonder* 13
Shields, Charles J., *Plague and Fire of London* 45
Shusterman, Neal, *Mindbenders: Stories to Warp Your Brain* 66
Shyer, Marlene Fanta, *Welcome Home, Jellybean* 44
Sidman, Joyce, *The World According to Dog: Poems and Teen Voices* 49
Sis, Peter, *Tibet Through the Red Book* 1
Skurzynski, Gloria, *Clones* 65
Skurzynski, Gloria, *Hunted* 40
Skurzynski, Gloria, *Spider's Voice* 25
Slavik, Diane, *Daily Life in Ancient and Modern Jerusalem* 37
Sleator, William, *Interstellar Pig* 65
Smith Roland, *The Captain's Dog: My Journey with the
　Lewis and Clark Tribe* 5
Smith, Roland, *Jaguar* 40
Snicket, Lemony, *The Bad Beginning* 32
Sones, Sonya, *What My Mother Doesn't Know* 74
Soto, Gary, *Taking Sides* 28
Speare, Elizabeth George, *Sign of the Beaver* 41
Speare, Elizabeth George, *The Witch of Blackbird Pond* 30
Spinelli, Jerry, *Maniac Magee* 52
Spinelli, Jerry, *Milkweed* 38
Spinelli, Jerry, *Wringer* 72
Stroud, Jonathan, *The Amulet of Samarkand* 3
Stroud, Jonathan, *The Golem's Eye* 3
Tashjian, Janet, *Tru Confessions* 44
Taylor, Theodore, *The Bomb* 65
Taylor, Theodore, *Sweet Friday Island* 70
Taylor, Theodore, *Timothy of the Cay* 70
Tekavec, Valerie, *Teenage Refugees from Bosnia-Herzegovina Speak Out* 23
Thesman, Jean, *The Other Ones* 15
Trueman, Terry, *Cruise Control* 69
Van Draanen, Wendelin, *Sammy Keyes and the Search for Snake Eyes* 43

Van Draanen, Wendelin, *Sammy Keyes and the Sisters of Mercy* 63
Viencenia-Saurez, Ana, *The Flight to Freedom* 19
Vornholt, John, *The Troll King* 47
Walters, Eric, *War of the Eagles* 39
White, Alana J., *Sacagawea: Westward with Lewis and Clark* 5
Whitesel, Cheryl Alyward, *Rebel: A Tibetan Odyssey* 1
Whytock, Cherry, *My Scrumptious Scottish Dumplings:*
   The Life of Angelica Cookson Potts 71
Wilmot-Buxton, E.M., *Viking Gods and Heroes* 27
Wolff, Virginia Euwer, *Bat 6* 39
Wolkstein, Diane, *Magic Orange Tree: And Other Haitian Folktales* 19
Woodruff, Joan Leslie, *The Shiloh Renewal* 69
Woodson, Jacqueline, *Last Summer with Maizon* 35
Worthen, Tom and Kyle Hernandez, *Broken Hearts…Healing:*
   Young Poets Speak Out on Divorce 11
Wrede, Patricia C., *Dealing With Dragons* 4
Yolen, Jane, *Queen's Own Fool* 25
Yolen, Jane and Bruce Coville, *Armageddon Summer* 55
Young, Ella, *Celtic Wonder Tales* 7
Zindel, Paul, *Loch* 75
Zindel, Paul, *Raptor* 75
Zindel, Paul, *Rats* 75
Zindel, Paul, *Reef of Death* 75

C. Titles

11,000 Years Lost, Griffin 36
Alanna: The First Adventure, Pierce 59
Aleutian Sparrow, Hesse 39
The Amazing Maurice and His Educated Rodents, Pratchett 60
Beekman's Big Deal, De Guzman 20
Behind the Mountains: The Diary of Celiane Esperance, Danticat 19
Blue Wolf, Creedon 15
Boston Jane: The Claim, Holm 42
Bud, Not Buddy, Curtis 16
Call Me Maria, Cofer 10
Contents Under Pressure, Zeises 74
Coraline, Gaiman 32
The Creek, Holm 43
The Dark Hills Divide, Carman 6
The Darkest Evening, Durbin 24
Deep, Vance 70
Dizzy, Cassidy 7
Dragon: Hound of Honor, Edwards and Hamilton 25
Duel, Grossman 37

The Final Reckoning, Jarvis 46
Friction, Frank 30
Gathering Blue, Lowry 50
Getting Near to Baby, Couloumbis 13
The Goblin Wood, Bell 3
The Golden Hour, Williams 73
Granny Torrelli Makes Soup, Creech 14
The Gravedigger's Cottage, Lynch 51
*A Hat Full of Sky: The Continuing Adventures of Tiffany Aching
    and the Wee Free Men*, Pratchett 61
Here Today, Martin 52
Hill Hawk Hattie, Clark 8
Hoot, Hiaasen 40
The House of the Scorpion, Farmer 26
Iqbal, D'Adamo 18
I've Already Forgotten Your Name, Philip Hall!, Greene 35
Joey Pigza Loses Control, Gantos 33
Kingdom of the Golden Dragon, Allende 1
Last Shot, Feinstein 28
Loser, Spinelli 67
Magyk, Sage 64
Multiple Choice, Tashjian 68
My Cup Runneth Over: The Life of Angelica Cookson Potts, Whytock 71
My Louisiana Sky, Holt 44
Night of the Bat, Zindel 75
Nine Days a Queen: The Short Life and Reign of Lady Jane Grey, Rinaldi . . .62
Oddballs, Sleator 66
The Oracle Betrayed, Fisher 29
The Other Side of Truth, Naidoo 56
Pagan's Vows, Jinks 48
Period Pieces: Stories for Girls, Deak and Embry Litchman, eds. 21
Petals in the Ashes, Hooper 45
Pictures of Hollis Woods, Giff 34
The Princess of Neptune, Dodd 22
Rebel, Roberts 63
The Revealers, Wilhelm 72
Ruby Electric, Nelson 57
*Sacajawea: The Story of Bird Woman and the Lewis and Clark
    Expedition*, Bruchac 5
Sam I Am, Cooper 12
The Sea of Trolls, Farmer 27
Shadows on the Sea, Harlow 38
Skellig, Almond 2
Snakes Don't Miss Their Mothers, Kerr 49
The Steps, Cohn 11

Stolen by the Sea, Myers 54
A Stone in My Hand, Clinton 9
Stuck in Neutral, Trueman 69
The Thief Lord, Funke 31
The Thorn Ogres of Hagwood, Jarvis 47
A Time To Love: Stories from the Old Testament, Myers 55
Under the Sun, Dorros 23
Virtual War, Skurzynski 65
The Watsons Go to Birmingham–1963, Curtis 17
Wild Man Island, Hobbs 41
The Wizard Test, Bell 4
Wolf Brother, Paver 58
Year of No Rain, Mead 53

D. Titles, Similar

*5 Novels: Alan Mendelsohn, The Boy From Mars, Slaves of Spiegel, The
 Last Guru, The Snarkout Boys and The Avocado of Death*, Pinkwater 22
19 Varieties of Gazelle: Poems of the Middle East, Nye 37
Abarat, Barker 46
Absolutely Normal Chaos, Creech 35
An Acceptable Time, L'Engle 73
After Hamelin, Richardson 60
The Alchemist's Cat, Jarvis 60
Aleutian Adventure: Kayaking in the Birthplace of the Winds, Bowermaster . . .39
*An American Spring: Sofia's Immigrant Diary, The North End of Boston,
 1903*, Lasky 14
Among the Hidden, Haddix 50
The Amulet of Samarkand, Stroud 3
The Ancient One, Barron 15
*Angus, Thongs, and Full-Frontal Snogging: Confession of
 Georgia Nicolson*, Rennison 71
Anybodies, Bode 51
Are You There God? It's Me, Margaret, Blume 30
Armageddon Summer, Yolen and Coville 55
The Art of Keeping Cool, Lisle 38
Artemis Fowl, Colfer 64
At the Sign of the Sugared Plum, Hooper 45
The Bad Beginning, Snicket 32
Bat 6, Wolff 39
Beatnik Rutabagas From Beyond the Stars, Dodd 22
Because of Winn Dixie, DiCamillo 52
Before We Were Free, Alvarez 19
Belle Teale, Martin 52
Beringia: Bridge of Spirits, Hoshikawa 58

The Best Christmas Pageant Ever, Robinson 12
The Best School Year Ever, Robinson 67
The BFG, Dahl 32
Black Angels, Murphy 17
Bloodsuckers: Bats, Bugs, and Other Bloodthirsty Creatures, Houghton 75
Blue Avenger Cracks the Code, Howe 31
Blue Heron, Avi 57
The Bomb, Taylor 65
A Bone From a Dry Sea, Dickinson 36
Book of the Lion, Cadnum 25
Born Too Short: The Confessions of an Eighth-Grade Basket Case, Elish ...66
Bosnia and Herzegovina, Gabrielpillai 23
Boston Jane: An Adventure, Holm 42
Boston Jane: Wilderness Days, Holm 42
Both Sides of Time, Cooney 73
The Boy Who Lost His Face, Sachar 67
The Breadwinner, Ellis 56
Bridge to Terabithia, Paterson 13
Broken Hearts…Healing: Young Poets Speak Out on Divorce, Worthen and
    Hernandez 11
The Bromeliad Trilogy: Truckers, Diggers, and Wings, Pratchett ...22
Buccaneers, Lawrence 70
Buddy is a Stupid Name for a Girl, Roberts 63
The Captain's Dog: My Journey with the Lewis and Clark Tribe, Smith 5
The Capture, Lasky 47
Cart and Cwidder, Jones 36
Case of the Missing Cutthroats, George 40
Catherine, Called Birdy, Cushman 48
Celtic Wonder Tales, Young 7
Chain of Fire, Naidoo 56
Chasing Vermeer, Baillett 34
City of the Beasts, Allende 1
The Clique, Harrison 71
Clones, Skurzynski 65
Close Kin, Dunkle 3
Coping in a Blended Family, Hurwitz 11
*Coping with ADD/ADHD (Attention Deficit Disorder/Attention Deficit
    Hyperactivity Disorder)*, Morrison 33
A Corner of the Universe, Martin 51
Counting Stars, Almond 2
Cruise Control, Trueman 69
The Crystal Prison, Jarvis 46
Cuba 15, Osa 19
Daily Life in Ancient and Modern Jerusalem, Slavik 37
Danger at the Fair, Kehret 63

The Dark Portal, Jarvis 46
Daughter of the Wind, Cadnum 27
Daughter of Venice, Napoli 31
Daughters of Fire: Heroines of the Bible, Manushkin 55
The Day My Butt Went Psycho, Griffiths 66
Dead Man in Indian Creek, Hahn 43
Dealing With Dragons, Wrede 4
Dear Mr. Henshaw, Cleary 16
The Divorce Express, Danziger 57
*Do You Remember the Color Blue?: Questions Children Ask
   About Being Blind*, Alexander 14
The Dolphin Project, Emmer 37
Don't Know Much About Kings and Queens of England, Davis 62
Doormat, McWilliams 74
The Dragon Rider, Funke 32
The Egyptian Box, Curry 29
Elijah's Angel: A Story for Chanukah and Christmas, Rosen 12
Elizabeth I and Tudor England, Greenblatt 62
Elizabeth I: Red Rose of the House of Tudor, England, 1544, Lasky 62
Ender's Game, Card 26
The Enemy Has a Face, Miklowitz 9
Equal Rites, Pratchett 61
Everything on a Waffle, Horvath 51
Everything You Need to Know About Cerebral Palsy, Pincus 69
Eye of the Changer: Northwest Indian Tale, Ringstad 42
The Eye, the Ear, and the Arm, Farmer 53
Fated Sky, Branford 27
The Fire Eaters, Almond 2
Fire on the Wind, Crew 8
The Flight to Freedom, Viencenia-Saurez 19
For All Time, Cooney 29
For the Life of Leatitia, Hodge 19
For the Love of Venice, Napoli 31
Forbidden City: A Novel of Modern Day China, Bell 1
The Forgotten Beasts of Eld, McKillip 4
*Free the Children: A Young Man Fights Against Child Labor and
   Proves That Children Can Change the World*, Keilburger 18
Frightful's Mountain, George 49
Frindle, Clements 67
From the Mixed-Up Files of Mrs. Basil E. Frankweiler, Konigsburg 20
Gallows Hill, Duncan 61
The Gentleman Outlaw and Me–Eli, Hahn 8
Get on Out of Here, Philip Hall!, Greene 35
Ghost Canoe, Hobbs 42
Ghost Stories of the Pacific Northwest, MacDonald 42

The Girl Death Left Behind, McDaniel 13
Girl in Blue, Rinaldi 8
A Girl Named Disaster, Farmer 53
Girl Stuff: A Survival Guide to Growing Up, Blackstone and Guest 21
The Giver, Lowry 50
Goddess of Yesterday, Cooney 29
Going Home, Mohr 10
The Golden Compass, Pullman 50
The Golem's Eye, Stroud 3
The Graduation of Jake Moon, Park 34
The Great Blue Yonder, Shearer 13
The Great Gilly Hopkins, Paterson 34
The Great Plague: The Diary of Alice Payton, London 1665-1666, Oldfield .. 45
*Great Storm: The Hurricane Diary of T.J. King, Galveston,
   Texas, 1900*, Rogers 54
Gregor the Overlander and the Prophecy of Bane, Collins 47
Habibi, Nye 37
Harris and Me: A Summer Remembered, Paulsen 66
Harry Potter and the Sorcerer's Stone, Rowling 64
Hatchet, Paulsen 41
Hattie on Her Way, Clark 8
Heads or Tails: Stories from the Sixth Grade, Gantos 33
Heaven Eyes, Almond 2
Helmi Mavis: A Finnish-American Girlhood, Biesanz 24
Himalaya, Neale 1
Hole in the Sky, Hautman 50
Holes, Sachar 43
The Hollow Kingdom, Dunkle 3
Hoopmania: The Book of Basketball History and Trivia, Herzog 28
House on Hound Hill, Prince 45
The House on Mango Street, Cisneros 30
How to Eat Fried Worms, Rockwell 67
Hunted, Skurzynski 40
Hurricane!, Nicolson 54
Hurricane and Tornado, Challoner 54
In the Hand of the Goddess, Pierce 59
Inkheart, Funke 31
Interstellar Pig, Sleator 65
Into the Land of the Unicorns, Coville 6
Into the Wild, Hunter 47
Iqbal Masih and the Crusaders Against Child Slavery, Kuklin 18
Island of the Blue Dolphins, O'Dell 13
*It's a Girl Thing: Straight Talk About First Bras, First Periods,
   and Your Changing Body*, Jukes 21
It's Not the End of the World, Blume 57

Jaguar, Smith 40
Jason's Miracle: A Hanukkah Story, Benderly 12
Joey Pigza Swallowed the Key, Gantos 33
John Riley's Daughter, Matthews 44
Joshua's Song, Harlow 18
*The Journal of Otto Peltonen: A Finnish Immigrant: Hibbing Minnesota,
    1905,* Durbin 24
Journey to Jo'burg: A South African Story, Naidoo 53
Journeys with Elijah: Eight Tales of the Prophet, Goldin 55
Julie, George 58
Julie of the Wolves, George 41
Just Like Martin, Davis 17
The Kin: Suth's Story, Dickinson 36
The Kindling, Armstrong 65
Kinship, Krisher 7
Kissing Doorknobs, Hesser 68
Kissing the Rain, Brooks 72
Lady Knight, Pierce 59
The Last Book in the Universe, Philbrick 26
The Last Holiday Concert, Clements 67
Last Summer with Maizon, Woodson 35
The Leopard Sword, Cadnum 48
Lionboy, Corder 58
Lioness Rampant, Pierce 59
Loch, Zindel 75
A Long Way From Chicago, Peck 14
Looking for Bobowicz: A Hoboken Chicken Story, Pinkwater 20
Losing Forever, Friesen 11
The Lost Years of Merlin, Barron 64
Love and Other Four Letter Words, Mackler 74
Magic Orange Tree: And Other Haitian Folktales, Wolkstein 19
Maniac Magee, Spinelli 52
Martin the Warrior, Jacques 46
Mary, Bloody Mary, Meyer 62
Matilda Bone, Cushman 48
A Matter of Profit, Bell 3
The Maze, Hobbs 40
The Meaning of Consuelo, Cofer 10
Melonhead, De Guzman 20
The Messenger, Lowry 50
A Midnight Clear: Family Christmas Stories, Paterson 12
Milkweed, Spinelli 38
Mindbenders: Stories to Warp Your Brain, Shusterman 66
The Mind's Eye, Fleischman 69
The Misfits, Howe 72

Molly Moon's Incredible Book of Hypnotism, Byng 32
Monsieur Eek, Ives 51
The Moves Make the Man, Brooks 28
Mrs. Frisby and the Rats of NIMH, O'Brien 46
My Name Was Keoko, Park 15
*My Scrumptious Scottish Dumplings: The Life of
    Angelica Cookson Potts*, Whytock 71
The Neverending Story, Ende 6
Nigeria, Murphy 56
Night Hoops, Deuker 28
The Night of Wishes, Ende 6
No More Dead Dogs, Korman 22
No Turning Back: A Novel of South Africa, Naidoo 56
Not as Crazy as I Seem, Harrar 68
Nzingha: Warrior Queen of Matamba, Angola, Africa, 1595, McKissack 53
Oasis, Hapka 36
Obsessive Compulsive Disorder, Hyman 68
Once Upon a Cuento, Miller-Lachmann 10
One Mom Too Many, Bryant 11
The Other Ones, Thesman 15
Our Only May Amelia, Holm 24
Out of Bounds: Seven Stories of Conflict and Hope, Naidoo 9
Out of the Dust, Hesse 16
Owl In Love, Kindl 15
Owl in the Office, Baglio 49
Pagan in Exile, Jinks 48
Pagan's Crusade, Jinks 48
Page, Pierce 59
PaperQuake: A Puzzle, Reiss 73
Parsifal's Page, Morris 25
Patience, Princess Catherine, Meyer 62
The People of Sparks, DuPrau 6
Perfectionism: What's Bad About Being Too Good?, Goldberg 68
*The Period Book: Everything You Don't Want to Ask
    (But Need to Know)*, Gravelle 21
Petey, Mikaelsen 69
Philip Hall Likes Me, I Reckon Maybe, Greene 35
The Pied Piper of Hamlin, Browning 60
Plague and Fire of London, Shields 45
Playing for Keeps, Nixon 70
Point Blank, Horowitz 65
The Princess Diaries, Cabot 71
Pulling Princes, O'Connell 71
*Putting On the Brakes: Young People's Guide to Understanding
    Attention Deficit Hyperactivity Disorder*, Quinn 33

Title	Page
Queen's Own Fool, Yolen	25
Raptor, Zindel	75
Rascal, North	49
Rats, Zindel	75
Rebel: A Tibetan Odyssey, Whitesel	1
Red Scarf Girl: A Memoir of the Cultural Revolution, Jiang	9
Redwall, Jacques	6
Reef of Death, Zindel	75
Religions of the World: The Illustrated Guide to Origins, Beliefs, Traditions and Festivals, Brueilly	7
Remember: The Journey to School Integration, Morrison	17
The Return of Gabriel, Armistead	17
The Root Cellar, Lunn	73
The Royal Kingdoms of Ghana, Mali and Songhay: Life in Medieval Africa, McKissack	53
Ruby Holler, Creech	34
The Ruby in the Smoke, Pullman	45
Sacagawea: Girl of the Shining Mountains, Roop	5
Sacagawea: Westward with Lewis and Clark, White	5
Saga of Lewis and Clark: Into the Uncharted West, Schmidt	5
Samir and Yonatan, Carmi	37
Sammy Keyes and the Search for Snake Eyes, Van Draanen	43
Sammy Keyes and the Sisters of Mercy, Van Draanen	63
Sarajevo: Natasha's Story, Nicholson	23
Scared Stiff, Roberts	43
Scorpions, Myers	72
Secret Heart, Almond	2
Shabanu: Daughter of the Wind, Fisher	18
Shadowmaker, Nixon	63
Shattered: Stories of Children and War, Armstrong	9
Shelter Dogs: Amazing Stories of Adopted Strays, Kehret	49
The Shiloh Renewal, Woodruff	69
Sign of the Beaver, Speare	41
Silent Boy, Lowry	2
Silent Dancing: A Partial Remembrance of a Puerto Rican Childhood, Cofer	10
Silent Storm, Garland	54
Silent to the Bone, Konigsburg	68
Simply Alice, Naylor	30
So You Want to Be a Wizard, Duane	4
Some Friend, Bradby	35
Song of Sampo Lake, Durbin	24
Sounder, Armstrong	16
The Spellcoats, Jones	58
Spider's Voice, Skurzynski	25
Sportswriting: A Beginner's Guide, Craig	28

Squire, Pierce 25
Stand Tall, Bauer 57
Step From Heaven, Na 15
Stepliving for Teens: Getting Along with Stepparents and Siblings, Block 11
Stepping on the Cracks, Hahn 38
Stitches, Huser 72
Stolen Dreams: Portraits of Working Children, Parker 18
The Story Atlas of the Bible, Hunter 55
Stranger Next Door, Kehret 20
Streams to the River, River to the Sea: A Novel of Sacajawea, O'Dell 5
Street Magic, Pierce 4
Summer of My German Soldier, Greene 38
Summer of the Swans, Byars 44
The Supernaturalist, Colfer 26
Sweet Friday Island, Taylor 70
A Swiftly Tilting Planet, L'Engle 26
Taking Sides, Soto 28
Tale of Despereaux: Being the Story of a Mouse, a Princess, Some Soup, and a Spool of Thread, DiCamillo 47
Tales from Watership Down, Adams 60
Tales of the Norse Gods, Picard 27
The Talisman, Ewing 29
Tangerine, Bloor 14
Teen Ink: A Collection of Short Stories, Art and Photography, Meyer 34
Teenage Refugees from Bosnia-Herzegovina Speak Out, Takavec 23
Teenage Refugees from Somalia Speak Out, Hussein 56
The Tent: A Parable in One Sitting, Paulsen 55
Terror from the Gulf: A Hurricane in Galveston, Jones 54
There's a Bat in Bunk Five, Danziger 7
There's an Owl in the Shower, George 40
They Took My Father: Finnish Americans in Stalin's Russia, Sevandar 24
Thin Wood Walls, Patneaude 39
Things Not Seen, Clements 22
This Place Has No Atmosphere, Danziger 20
This Side of Paradise, Layne 26
Thura's Diary: My Life in Wartime Iraq, Al-Windawi 9
Tibet Through the Red Book, Sis 1
Tiger Rising, DiCamillo 13
Timespinners, Gray 36
Timothy of the Cay, Taylor 70
To Kill a Mockingbird, Lee 30
Too Old For This, Too Young For That!: Your Survival Guide For the Middle-School Years, Mosatche 21
Touching Spirit Bear, Mikaelsen 41
A Young Adult's Guide to Building a Jewish Life, Feinstein 12

The Transall Saga, Paulsen ...73
The Troll King, Vornholt ...47
Troubling a Star, L'Engle ...43
Tru Confessions, Tashjian ...44
The True Confessions of Charlotte Doyle, Avi ...8
The True Meaning of Cleavage, Fredericks ...74
Twisted Summer, Roberts ...63
Under Copp's Hill, Ayer ...14
Vendela in Venice, Bjork ...31
A View from Saturday, Konigsburg ...52
Views from Our Shoes: Growing Up with a Brother or Sister with Special Needs, Meyer ...44
Viking, Margeson ...27
Viking Gods and Heroes, Wilmot-Buxton ...27
Waiting for Dolphins, Crowe ...70
Waiting for Odysseus, McLaren ...29
Walk Two Moons, Creech ...16
The Walking Stones, Hunter ...7
War of the Eagles, Walters ...39
Warriors Don't Cry, Beals ...17
Watership Down, Adams ...60
The Wee Free Men, Pratchett ...61
A Week in the Woods, Clements ...41
Welcome Home, Jellybean, Shyer ...44
Welcome Home or Someplace Like It, Agell ...38
What Hearts, Brooks ...57
What My Mother Doesn't Know, Sones ...74
What Would Joey Do?, Gantos ...33
When Zachary Beaver Came to Town, Holt ...52
The Whipping Boy, Fleischman ...16
Why Does the Coqui Sing?, Polikoff ...10
A Wind Is Not a River, Griese ...39
The Witch of Blackbird Pond, Speare ...30
Witches Abroad, Pratchett ...61
A Wizard Alone, Duane ...64
A Wizard of Earthsea, Le Guin ...4
The Wizard's Apprentice, Koller ...64
Wolf-Speaker, Pierce ...58
The Wolves in the Walls, Gaiman ...32
The Woman Who Rides Like a Man, Pierce ...59
The Wonderful Story of Henry Sugar and Six More, Dahl ...66
The World According to Dog: Poems and Teen Voices, Sidman ...49
Wringer, Spinelli ...72
Wyrd Sisters, Pratchett ...61

A Year Down Yonder, Peck 51
Year of Secret Assignments, Moriarty 74
Yikes!: A Smart Girl's Guide to Surviving Tricky, Sticky,
  Icky Situations, Holyoke 21
Young People from Bosnia Talk about War, Fireside .23
Zlata's Diary: A Child's Life in Sarajevo, Filipovic 23

E. Subjects

Accidents 43, 51
African Americans 16, 17, 35, 73
Africans 53, 56
Alcoholism 33, 70
Animals 6, 15, 46, 49, 51, 58, 75
Artists 34, 37, 57
Attention Deficit Hyperactivity Disorder 33
Baseball 24, 33
Basketball 28
Bats 75
Birds 38, 40
Brothers 17, 31
Brothers and Sisters 9, 12, 22, 24, 27, 47, 51, 53, 56, 57, 59, 66, 73, 74
Bullies 20, 40, 52, 67, 72
Cats 6, 46, 49, 60
Child Abuse 18
Child Neglect 7
Child Sexual Abuse 30
Communism 24
Cooking 14, 42, 45, 71
Crime 1, 6, 28, 31, 37, 38, 43, 48, 56, 62, 63, 70
Death 13, 23, 39, 43, 44, 45, 51, 56, 58, 75
Depression, The 16
Disabilities 14, 44, 50, 65, 68, 69
Divorce 10, 11, 57, 69
Dogs 25, 41, 49, 63
Drugs 7, 26
Ecology 36, 40
Elderly 34, 36, 37, 52, 63, 73
Emotional Problems 17, 30, 48, 51, 68, 69
Endangered Species, 40
Extraterrestrials 22
Family Problems 2, 9, 13, 17, 44, 52, 55, 57, 69, 70, 74
Fathers and Daughters 6, 8, 10, 11, 49, 51, 54
Fathers and Sons 15, 20, 26, 33, 41, 58, 67, 69, 75
Fires 7, 45

Folklore 5, 15, 27, 58, 60
Foster Homes, 16, 34
Friendship 1, 2, 3, 4, 14, 20, 25, 28, 30, 31, 35, 36, 37, 38, 40, 43, 44, 48, 52, 57, 58, 61, 63, 66, 71, 72, 73
Frontier and Pioneer Life 5, 8, 42
Gambling 28
Ghosts 46
Goblins 3
Gods and Goddesses 27, 29
Grandfathers 16
Grandmothers 1, 11, 12, 14, 17, 35, 38, 44, 63
Grieving 3, 4, 8, 13, 15, 16, 25, 31, 41, 49, 50, 51, 56, 58, 73
Haitians 19
Holidays 12, 49
Illness 39, 45
Immigrants 19
Infants 2, 13, 45, 64
Internment Camps 39
Jewish Americans 12
Jews 37
Journeys 5, 6, 16, 17, 22, 23, 27, 36, 53, 58, 73
Kidnapping 1, 7, 27, 64, 70
Knights and Knighthood 3, 25, 48, 59
Korean Americans 15
Magic 1, 3, 4, 6, 15, 27, 31, 36, 46, 47, 58, 59, 60, 61, 64
Medical Experimentation 26, 65
Menstruation 21
Mental Illness 43
Mexican Americans 54
Mice 46
Middle Ages 25, 48
Mothers and Daughters 7, 21, 32, 44, 52, 62, 71
Mothers and Sons 4, 5, 23
Moving 2, 10, 19, 20, 24, 39, 40, 51, 57
Murder 18, 25, 29, 43, 56, 62, 70
Music 15, 16, 22, 24, 60
Native Americans 5, 39, 42
Natural Disasters 54
Occupations 4, 8, 18, 27, 28, 50, 59, 70, 71
Orphans 16, 31, 34, 42, 48, 50, 54, 64
Pets, 49, 51
Photography 37
Prehistoric Man 36, 58
Prejudices 3, 4, 12, 17, 23, 24, 44, 52, 72
Puerto Rican Americans 10

Race Relations 5, 9, 10, 17
Rats 46, 60
Refugees 23, 53, 56
Relationships 35, 42, 55, 74
Religion 1, 2, 9, 12, 29, 48, 55, 62
Runaways 16, 31, 34, 40
Schools 12, 20, 22, 30, 39, 52, 57, 67, 68, 71, 72
Self-Esteem 8, 29, 34, 35, 42, 47, 54, 67, 68, 71
Self-Identity 4, 7, 15, 16, 18, 26, 32, 44, 50, 59, 64, 65, 69
Sexual Assault 23
Sexuality 21, 30, 59, 74
Sisters 13, 36, 45
Stepfamilies 11
Survival 18, 23, 24, 36, 41, 46, 53, 54, 58
Teachers 19, 22, 30, 48
Time Travel 36, 73
Track and Field 15
Violence 9, 19, 23, 24, 46, 47, 53, 56, 58, 62, 75
War 4, 23, 38, 39, 53, 65
Weight Control 71
Witchcraft 3, 47, 61
Wizards 4, 27, 64
Wolves 15, 58
World War 12, 38, 39
Writing 10, 19, 28, 57, 70, 72

F. Genres

Adventure 1, 27, 36, 41, 54, 59
Fantasy 1, 2, 3, 4, 6, 15, 27, 29, 32, 36, 46, 47, 49, 58, 59, 60, 61, 64, 73
Historical 5, 8, 16, 17, 24, 25, 36, 37, 38, 39, 42, 44, 45, 48, 52, 54, 62, 73
Horror 32, 46, 75
Humor 11, 22, 33, 35, 37, 40, 61, 66, 71
International 1, 2, 7, 9, 11, 18, 19, 23, 24, 25, 27, 31, 37, 45, 46, 48, 53, 56, 62, 70, 71, 75
Multicultural 1, 5, 9, 10, 12, 14, 15, 16, 17, 18, 19, 21, 23, 24, 26, 35, 39, 42, 48, 53, 54, 55, 56, 72, 73
Mystery 1, 22, 25, 28, 29, 31, 37, 38, 40, 41, 43, 48, 63, 70
Realistic 7, 9, 10, 11, 12, 13, 14, 18, 19, 20, 21, 23, 28, 30, 33, 34, 35, 40, 43, 51, 56, 57, 63, 67, 68, 69, 70, 71, 72, 74
Science Fiction 22, 26, 50, 65
Short Stories 21, 55, 66
Sports 15, 28, 33

Supernatural 2, 36, 46, 58

G. Curriculum Connections

Art 34, 47, 55, 57
Career Education 28
Foreign Languages 10
Health 1, 2, 14, 30, 33, 43, 44, 68, 69, 71, 74
Language Arts 6, 10, 11, 13, 15, 21, 25, 28, 32, 47, 57, 60, 61, 66, 67
Math 20, 27, 53, 70
Physical Education 28, 35
Science 1, 4, 6, 22, 26, 29, 33, 40, 41, 46, 47, 49, 50, 58, 63, 69, 75
Social Studies 3, 5, 7, 8, 9, 11, 12, 15, 16, 17, 18, 19, 23, 24, 27, 29, 31, 36, 37, 38, 39, 42, 45, 48, 51, 52, 53, 54, 56, 59, 60, 62, 63, 64, 65, 70, 72, 73

Appendix
Student Evaluation Form

On the next page is the form I use in my graduate level Young Adult Literature course. They add their five book titles.

Booktalk Evaluation Form

Date: _____ Grade: _____ Subject: _____ M or F (circle one)

Booktalk Topic: _____

                                                           (circle one)

1. Did you enjoy listening to the booktalks?   Y   N

2. Have you ever listened to a booktalk before?   Y   N

3. Would you like to hear more booktalks?   Y   N

4. Which one of the following was your *favorite* type of booktalk?
    A. First person (when I talked like one of the characters in the book)
    B. Excerpt (when I read aloud a portion of the book)
    C. Discussion (when I just talked about the book)

5. Which one of the following was your *least favorite* type of booktalk?
    A. First person (when I talked like one of the characters in the book)
    B. Excerpt (when I read aloud a portion of the book)
    C. Discussion (when I just talked about the book)

6. Of the five books that were booktalked, which one are you *most* likely to read?

7. Of the five books that were booktalked, which one are you *least* likely to read?

8. What do you usually read? (circle as many as apply)
    A. Magazines
    B. Newspapers
    C. Graphic novels
    D. Fiction (circle as many fiction genres as apply)

        Horror   Science Fiction   Fantasy   Historical   Romance

        Short Stories   Mysteries   Realistic

    E. Game Materials

www.ingramcontent.com/pod-product-compliance
Lightning Source LLC
Chambersburg PA
CBHW060514300426
44112CB00017B/2671